The Age of Giant Mammals

Illustrated by
James G. Teason

THE AGE OF

GIANT MAMMALS

Daniel Cohen

DODD, MEAD & COMPANY · NEW YORK

To my oldest friends Harry and Arlene Hirsch,
and to Danny and Susie

Introduction

CARTOONS and comic strips about cave men usually show them living in a world full of dinosaurs. This is what you might call poetic license. Dinosaurs died out 70 million years ago; man has been around for perhaps a million years.

Ever since the dinosaurs were discovered during the last century we have all become very dinosaur conscious. Indeed, we have been so hypnotized by the giant reptiles that we have almost overlooked the fact that our own ancestors really did live in a world of giant animals. These were the giant mammals, and many of them rivaled the dinosaurs in size and strangeness. Our own ancestors probably dined upon woolly mammoth and if they were careless or unlucky they may have been dined upon by saber-toothed cats.

Elephants of various sorts tramped the world from the high Arctic to the tropics. There were rhinoceroses with thick fur coats, camels as tall as giraffes, beavers as big as bears, deer with antlers that measured ten feet from tip to tip and many other enormous creatures that never could have squeezed into Noah's ark.

Most of the giants have died. Some of their bones became buried and were fossilized. When the fossils were dug up thousands of years later, men could no longer remember that these giant animals had ever lived. So they told one another tales of giant men, and of dragons and unicorns, to explain the bones.

In the chapters that follow we will examine these "giants," "dragons," and "unicorns" from several angles: how they were discovered, what they were, how they evolved, the way they lived, and how and when most of them died. We will also look at the modern survivors of the age of giants.

Contents

The Age of Giant Mammals

1

Discovery of the Giants

IN 1577 SOME huge bones were dug up under an oak tree near
Lucerne, Switzerland. Despite their size the bones looked like
those of a man. The local authorities were in a quandary over how
they should be disposed of. Should an inquest be held into the cause
of the man's death? Should the incomplete skeleton be given a
proper Christian burial?

To help resolve the problem Dr. Felix Plater of the city of Basel,
a physician who was considered one of the most learned anatomists
of his day, was asked to examine the skeleton. The bones, said Dr.
Plater, were human, but they were those of a giant who had stood
some nineteen feet tall. The doctor even made a drawing of the
giant, and from this drawing the painter Johann Bock produced a
picture which showed a brawny bearded giant, clad only in leaves
and carrying a tree in one hand and a hapless human victim in the
other. The creature in the Bock painting is now known to be purely
imaginary, but in 1577 few doubted that such a giant had once lived
in the vicinity of Lucerne.

Dr. Plater's identification solved a problem for the Lucerne
authorities. Giants were not Christians, so there was no need to
rebury the bones. Instead they were put on display in the town hall.
The "Giant of Lucerne" became quite famous, and residents of the
town delighted in showing visitors the remains of their local giant.
The giant was even included in the coat of arms of Lucerne.

The bones lay in the Lucerne town hall for nearly two centuries.

13

Then one day they were seen by Johann Friedrich Blumenbach, a German zoologist. Within a few minutes Blumenbach identified them as the bones of a mammoth, an extinct variety of elephant. Convincing the citizens of Lucerne that their famous giant was really an extinct elephant and not the human brute in the Bock picture was no easy task. Yet elephants of one sort or another had lived near Lucerne, and near Los Angeles and London and Paris and New York and Moscow and Mexico City and a lot of other unlikely places. They were still living in many of these places a mere 10,000 years ago.

Near the castle of Chaumont in France, on January 11, 1613, workmen unearthed another set of enormous bones. Large bones must have turned up in that area regularly for, since ancient times, it had been known as *Champ des Géants* (Street of the Giants). These bones fell into the hands of a surgeon named Mazurier who lost no time in putting them on display for a fee. He told a remarkable story about how the bones had been taken from a brick tomb thirty feet long, twelve feet wide, and eight feet high. The man whose bones were found in the tomb had been twenty-five feet tall and ten feet across the shoulders, Mazurier declared. In addition, he knew the name of this giant, for the top of the tomb contained the inscription "Teutobochus Rex," indicating that the bones were those of Teutobochus, an ancient barbarian king who had been defeated and captured by the Roman general Caius Marius in the battle of Aquae Sextiae in 102 B.C. According to the Roman account this Teutobochus had been a man of gigantic stature.

Mazurier traveled around Europe for five years showing the bones. Unfortunately, he no longer had the complete skeleton, for "most of the bones after exposure to the air from 8:00 A.M. to 6:00 P.M. had crumbled to powder," he said.

The Teutobochus story was violently attacked by French naturalist Jean Riolan who asserted that Mazurier had purchased the bones from workmen and made up the details about their being

14

The giant of Lucerne

found in a tomb. Angry pamphlets were issued by supporters of both sides. As it turned out, Riolan was right; Mazurier was a faker. Two centuries later the bones were identified as those of a *dinotherium* ("huge beast"), an ancient elephant-like creature. "Teutobochus' bones" were finally properly housed in a Paris museum.

In 1645 at Hundssteigh, near Krems in Austria, troops digging trenches there uncovered a cache of ancient bones and teeth that were thought to be human. The discoverers were stunned by the size of these bones and even more amazed by the teeth. One of them wrote: ". . . The actual size of the predicted body is incredible; the head alone is as large as a round table, the arms as thick as the body of a man, and one tooth alone weighs five and one half pounds." Incredible, indeed. Imagine the size of a man from whom a single tooth weighed five and one half pounds!

15

Although these bones have been scattered throughout various collections and most of them were lost before scientists got a chance to examine them, drawings indicate that they must have belonged to a mammoth, an animal which had extraordinarily large teeth even for its size.

In Vienna the thigh bone of a mammoth was dug up in 1443 during excavations for the foundations of St. Stephen's Cathedral. The bone was hung above one of the gates of the Cathedral and for that reason people called the gate the "giant's gate." This bone ultimately found a home in the Geological Institute of Vienna University where it was correctly identified. After the bone was removed the name of the gate must have confused visitors since it was the smallest of the Cathedral's three gates.

"Giants' bones" were not limited to Europe. When the Spanish conquered Mexico they came upon the vast ruined city of Teotihuacán. The Aztecs who ruled Mexico at the time of the coming of the Spanish did not know who had built the city. When the Spanish asked them, the Aztecs said it had been built by giants. As proof they displayed the fossil bones of elephants that had been dug up in the vicinity.

The earliest known reference to giant bones was made by the Greek traveler and historian, Herodotus, who lived in the fifth century B.C. He told the story of a blacksmith at the city of Tegea in southern Greece who found the bones of a giant while digging a well. The giant, said Herodotus, was about twenty feet tall. This skeleton was most probably that of a large extinct mammal, but the Spartans decided that it was the skeleton of the legendary Orestes, son of Agamemnon. The Spartans had a reason for making this particular identification. They had been told in a prophecy that they would be victorious in war if they possessed the bones of Orestes, so they stole the great skeleton. Unfortunately, these bones have been lost. It would be interesting to know just what creature had inspired this early legend.

Huge bones from unknown animals must have been unearthed with fair regularity throughout Greek and Roman times. The Greek philosopher Pausanias identified a large skeleton dug up in the vicinity of Miletus in southern Greece as belonging to the Homeric hero Ajax. The Roman writer Suetonius noted that the Emperor Augustus (63 B.C. to A.D. 14) had a collection of large bones in his villa at Capri.

Practically every nation has developed its own stories of giants. Usually they are pictured as brutish creatures that prospered on the earth before the coming of man and perhaps contested with man and the gods for supremacy in the earliest days. Many of these legends doubtless began when men found gigantic bones and did not know what to make of them.

The legend of Polyphemus, the one-eyed giant who plays such an important part in Homer's *Odyssey*, almost certainly began with the discovery of elephant skulls. The skulls are oddly shaped and have a large hole in the center. This hole is really a nasal passage but in a way it looks very much like a single enormous eye socket. An Austrian paleontologist, Othenio Abel, theorized: "Sailors of Homeric days, blown off their course and finding such skulls in caves on the coast of Sicily, had never seen elephants. Hence, they hit on the idea that the skulls must be those of huge beings with one great eye in the middle of the forehead. Thus, the myth of the one-eyed Cyclops probably originated as, indeed, most legends of giants are based on finds of large primordial mammals."

The ancient Greek philosopher Empedocles (fifth century B.C.), upon viewing the fossil skull of an elephant, came to the conclusion that he was gazing upon the skull of Polyphemus.

Two thousand years later man's knowledge of fossil bones had not increased very much. In the fourteenth century the Italian writer Giovanni Boccaccio, best known as author of the *Decameron*, came to the same conclusion when shown an elephant skull which had been discovered at Trapani in western Sicily. In his book,

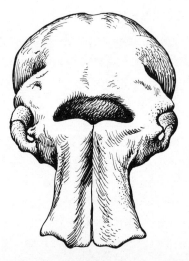

Skull of a mammoth, often mistaken for the skull of the mythical
one-eyed Cyclops

On the Genealogies of the Gods, Boccaccio estimated that the Cyclops must have been 300 feet tall.

The island of Sicily was rich in ancient elephant bones. They were still being dug up in the seventeenth century. An elephant skull was examined by Father Athanasius Kircher, an erudite man and respected scientific thinker who had made a special trip to Sicily to see the skull. Father Kircher came to the same conclusion as Empedocles and Boccaccio. He did disagree with Boccaccio's size estimate, however, and asserted that the Cyclops had been a mere thirty feet tall. Indeed, Father Kircher who was an expert on caves asserted that all large bones found underground were either those of giants or dragons.

Father Kircher was a Jesuit and no religious man of the seventeenth century was surprised or disconcerted by giants' bones because there are many references to giants in the Bible. In Genesis (6:4) there is the statement: "There were giants in the earth in those days." Later, in Numbers (13:33), is the report of the Israelites who had been sent ahead to spy on the inhabitants of the Promised Land: "And there we saw the giants, the sons of Anak, which came of the giants; and we were in our own sight as grasshoppers, and so we were in their sight." Upon hearing the report that the land for which they sought was inhabited by such frightful creatures, "All the congregation lifted up their voice, and cried; and the people wept that night."

But Scripture makes clear that in the time of the Israelites the giants were already a dying race. "For only Og, king of Bashan remained of the remnant of the giants; behold, his bedstead was a bedstead of iron; is it not in Rabbath of the children of Ammon? Nine cubits was the length thereof, and four cubits the breadth of it, and after the cubit of a man." (Deuteronomy 3:11). In modern measurements Og's bedstead would have been some thirteen feet long and six feet wide. Not a bed for a very large giant, but a giant nonetheless.

And, or course, who can ignore the most famous Biblical giant of all, Goliath, slain by the boy David? Goliath was a giant of believable size. The Old Testament gives his height as "six cubits and a span." Translated into modern measurements, he would have been somewhere between nine and eleven feet tall. But he was reputed to be very strong, even for his size. The Old Testament indicates he wore some 200 pounds of brass armor.

Giants presented no problems to the orthodox. Some got the idea that all men were descended from giants. In the Bible, the Patriarchs of the Old Testament all lived exceptionally long lives. Thus, it was not unnatural to assume that since they were greater than ordinary men they were also exceptionally tall—indeed, that they were giants. Early in the eighteenth century one writer figured out that Adam was 123 feet, nine inches in height, Noah a shade over 100 feet, and so on. Size and life span shrank progressively as one got closer to modern times.

Not all bones dug up out of the ground were interpreted as belonging to humanoid giants. There were tales of other kinds of giants as well. In the mythology of the Sioux Indians who lived in

South Dakota was the legend of the Thunder Beast. These great beasts were supposed to leap out of the storm clouds in times of famine and drive the buffalo herds to the Sioux hunters. In support of their story the Indians showed doubters the large jawbone of an unknown animal. They said that after every storm such bones were washed up out of the ground. In 1875 the American paleontologist Othniel Charles Marsh was shown one of these jawbones. He immediately recognized it as belonging to an ancient and previously unknown mammal of gigantic stature. Marsh gave the creature the Latin scientific name of *Brontotherium* which translated means "thunder beast."

At least some of the dragon legends which exist throughout the world must have originated with the finding of the bones of extinct giant mammals. Throughout most of Europe the dragon was belived to be an evil creature. But in China where the legend was particularly important the dragon was considered a symbol of good luck. Dragons were also known as bringers of rain, perhaps because after a heavy rain fossil bones that had been buried would be washed down from hillsides or exposed on the surface.

The Chinese even had their dragons classified by the number of toes they possessed. The imperial dragon had five toes, while the ordinary dragon had only four. The Japanese dragon was forced to hobble along on a mere three toes.

Although dragons no longer roamed the earth, the Chinese knew that their bones were scattered in various places. Until fairly recent times Chinese drug stores sold what they labeled dragon bones and teeth. These were ground up for medicinal purposes. Western travelers in China occasionally bought the strange bones and when they were examined by scientists they turned out to be the fossil remains of extinct mammals like mammoths, mastodons, and saber-toothed cats.

The fossil bones of the huge cave bears of Ice Age times played an important role in the dragon myths of Europe. Throughout the mountains of Central Europe there are innumerable "dragon caves" and "dragon grottos." In 1673 a German physician Patersonius Hayn explored some of these caves in the Little Carpathians in Hungary. He found several strange skulls which he identified as belonging to dragons. Hayn wrote a learned paper on the subject of "Dragon Skulls in the Carpathians."

Similar finds in Transylvanian caves inspired a German naturalist named Vollgnad to write an article on "Transylvanian Dragons." Although the drawings of the bones that accompanied this article show clearly that Vollgnad had been looking at the bones of cave bears, he somehow got the idea that his Transylvanian dragons could fly. So onto the traditional reptilian body of the dragon Vollgnad appended little bat-like wings.

The dragon

21

Father Kircher, who had reduced the size of the Cyclops to thirty feet, also had a theory about dragons. They still lived in caves beneath the earth, he believed. That is why their bones were commonly found underground. Those rare dragons that were seen on the surface, like the one that had the misfortune of running across St. George, were wanderers who had accidentally blundered into the sunlit world, and were prevented from returning underground, perhaps because an earthquake blocked the entrance to their cave.

Cave bears were not the only ancient mammals mistaken for dragons. At Klagenfurt in Austria the skull of a "dragon" was unearthed in the middle of the sixteenth century. The find inspired town officials to erect a monument which was completed and set up in the market place in 1590. It shows a giant killing a dragon. The body of the dragon is the traditional winged reptile of the dragon myth, but the head displays some oddly unreptilian features. To paleontologists the Klangenfurt dragon had a head that was shaped like that of an Ice Age mammal, the woolly rhinoceros. The original "dragon" skull which inspired the monument was kept on display in the town hall. When paleontologists examined the skull, it did indeed prove to have belonged to a woolly rhinoceros.

Even the unicorn, the fabulous one-horned beast mentioned in the Bible comes into the story of the finding of the bones of giant mammals. Although the unicorn was not regarded as a particularly large beast, when Europeans began unearthing the bones of elephants, they were often labeled as the bones and horns of unicorns.

While the Chinese used powdered "dragon bones" and "dragon teeth" as a cure for all diseases, Europeans of the seventeenth and eighteenth centuries put the same faith in powdered "unicorn horn." No well-stocked pharmacy or apothecary was without its supply of unicorn horn. To this day the unicorn is the animal symbol for the apothecaries' guild.

"Unicorn horn" was an expensive medicine, but still there was a great demand for it. No one can estimate the number of valuable

Unicorn skeleton reconstructed from mammoth bones

fossils that were ground up and swallowed by wealthy invalids.

The first known attempt to reconstruct an entire skeleton from fossil bones took place in 1663. Workers in a gypsum quarry near Quedlinburg, Germany, unearthed a cache of mammoth bones. These were turned over to Otto von Guericke, the Mayor of Magdenburg and also a scientist of considerable note who invented the vacuum pump. When he rearranged the elephant bones according to the beliefs of the times, von Guericke came up with the skeleton of a unicorn—at least part of the skeleton, for he did not seem able to find the right sort of bones to make the hind legs.

Nearly a century later von Guericke's unicorn was still considered an accurate reconstruction. The philosopher Leibniz approved it and published a drawing of it in his *Protogoea* published in 1749.

In 1720 Captain Tabbert von Strahelenberg of the Swedish army saw a large number of mammoth bones while he was being held prisoner of war in northern Russia. He tried to draw a picture of the

23

beast the bones must have belonged to and he came up with a picture of the unicorn.

Yet another Biblical creature which became involved in the story of the discovery of giant mammals was the great behemoth described in the Book of Job (40:15-24): "Behold now behemoth, which I made with thee; he eateth grass as an ox. Lo now, his strength is in his loins, and his force in the navel of his belly. He moveth his tail like a cedar; the sinews of his stones are wrapped together. His bones are as strong as pieces of brass; his bones are like bars of iron."

This could be a poetic description of almost any large plant-eating animal, but the rest of the description makes fairly clear that behemoth was really the water-loving hippopotamus, a creature the ancient Hebrews had undoubtedly seen during their captivity in Egypt and which may well have inhabited the rivers of Palestine in Biblical times. "Behold he drinketh up a river, and hasteth not: he trusteth that he can draw up Jordan into his mouth. He taketh it with his eyes: his nose pierceth through snares."

Behemoth, which is described as drawing up the river Jordan into his mouth, was moved to the Arctic in later centuries. Mammoth bones were particularly common in Siberia. The tusks from these fossil elephants formed an important trade item for Siberian cossacks. Perhaps one-third of all commercial ivory in the world comes from the tusks of these long dead mammals. The resemblance of the tusks found in Siberia to the tusks of living elephants should have been obvious, but most people in Russia had never seen a living elephant. In 1692 Nicolaus Cornelius Witzen who had been Dutch ambassador to Moscow and had gathered all the information he could on the Siberian mammoths wrote:

"The tale is told here that these teeth are the horns of the beast behemoth, which the Russians call mammut or mammoth, of which mention is made in the Book of Job. The animal is said to live underground now and thus break off its horns, namely those teeth that are found. Its color is supposed to be dark brown. It is said to be seldom seen, and when it does become visible the sight portends great misfortune."

Witzen himself did not believe this tale of the underground behemoth. He noted that the horns of the beast looked very much like the tusks of elephants. But most Russians of the seventeenth century believed behemoth was living a mole-like existence in northern Siberia. When the complete frozen carcass of a mammoth was found in 1714 one Russian scientist unhesitatingly identified it as the behemoth of the Bible.

Not all persons who came upon the remains of the mammoth felt obliged to offer a fantastic explanation for its existence. A mammoth tusk reportedly weighing 500 pounds was unearthed near the town of Hall in Swabia. Swabia was rich in fossils and the people had become blasé about even the biggest of them. They hung the enormous tusk on the wall of St. Michael's Church. Next to it they placed a bit of verse which asked, "Now say, my friend, what I may be."

Occasionally elephant bones were recognized for what they were, but people were at a loss to explain how the bones got to a place where there were no elephants.

An English antiquarian named Conyers discovered some elephant bones near London in 1716. Alongside the bones were some crudely chipped stone arrowheads. It seemed incredible that elephants had ever lived in London, and some persons suggested that the bones must be the recent remains of a beast that had escaped from a circus.

But one of Conyers' more educated associates said that the elephant must have been one of those brought over to Britain by the Roman Emperor Claudius under whose reign (A.D. 41 to 54) Britain was added to the Roman Empire. The sharpened stone, the man suggested, was part of a weapon made by the early Britons to kill the elephants of the Roman invaders.

25

In light of the knowledge of the time this suggestion seemed the most logical one, despite the fact that there was no indication that the Romans had ever brought elephants to Britain. Conyers put the bones and the stones in a cabinet with the label: "Find from Roman times."

Yet another giant animal of the Bible, leviathan, was once actually assembled from the bones of real giants. Of leviathan the Book of Job (41:9-10) says: "Shall not one be cast down even at the sight of him? None is so fierce that dare stir him up."

The identification of the animal that inspired leviathan is uncertain. Most scholars think it was a large crocodile. Yet another mention of leviathan (Psalms 104:25-26) makes the creature sound more like a sea-going animal than the swamp-dwelling crocodile: "So is this great and wide sea, wherein are things creeping innumerable, both small and great beasts. There go the ships, there is that leviathan, whom thou has made to play therein."

It is this passage that has made many identify leviathan with one of the great whales, although it is hard to see how the ancient Hebrews could have had much contact with large whales.

The idea that leviathan was some sort of real marine creature was firmly held by most people. Thus, as late as the nineteenth century when someone announced that he had unearthed the bones of leviathan, the public was ready to believe him.

During the 1840's an enormous skeleton, some 114 feet long and weighing 7,500 pounds was being exhibited throughout the United States by a German immigrant, Albert Koch. Koch called himself a doctor, but there is no indication that he merited the title. Not only did Koch assert that his creature was the Biblical leviathan, but also that it was the sea serpent of so many sailors' stories. To make the find more scientific Koch gave his monster a Latin name—*Hydrarchus*, meaning "water king."

If such a beast had ever lived it undoubtedly would have been king of the waters, but *Hydrarchus* was a clever forgery concocted

26

out of fossil bones dug up in Alabama. Koch had strung together parts of skeletons from several creatures to get a monster long enough to induce people to pay money to see it. The basic skeleton, particularly the fearsome head with its huge teeth, came from a fossil whale called *Zeuglodon*. The remains of five *Zeuglodons* must have been used in the fabrication of *Hydrarchus*.

Koch was the most successful swindler in paleontological history. A few years earlier he had sold a skeleton of "behemoth of the Bible" to Frederick William IV of Prussia. This, too, had been compounded out of the skeletons of several fossil whales.

Koch began his career as a fossil forger early in the year 1840 when he unearthed some mastodon bones on the bank of a small river in Missouri. Koch was a fossil hunter of considerable skill and he excavated the bones with great care. But when it came to assembling the complete skeleton he did it in a most extraordinary way. He put the huge curved tusks atop the creature's skull so that they looked like horns. Since he had found the bones of more than one mastodon, he simply added them all to the same skeleton. The result was a colossal and very formidable looking skeleton. He called his "discovery" *Missourium* or "Missouri animal." In 1840 mastodon skeletons were commonplace, but *Missourium* created a sensation.

The Koch skeleton was received fairly well by professional paleontologists, but in 1840 the science was still in its infancy. Dr. Richard Harlan, one of America's leading authorities of fossils, called *Missourium* "one of the most extensive and remarkable collections of fossil bones of extinct mammals which have hitherto been brought to light in this country." Harlan did, however, observe that the bones had been assembled in a rather strange way and he hoped that "Doctor" Koch would correct the errors. Gideon Mantell, the Englishman who discovered the first known dinosaur, *Iguanodon,* was even more enthusiastic: "It is the largest of all hitherto known fossil mammals—thirty feet long and fifteen feet in height."

27

The British Museum bought this concoction of bones for what was a staggering price at the time—two thousand dollars down and a thousand dollars a year for the rest of Koch's life. He collected twenty-three thousand dollars on the agreement. Making those annual payments must have galled the museum, for as soon as the laboratory workers got a close look at the bones they realized that they had been swindled. After a great deal of work the British Museum finally managed to salvage one fairly complete mastodon skeleton out of *Missourium*.

So it was as giants, dragons, unicorns, the behemoth, the sea serpent, and Roman elephants that modern man first confronted the remains of the giant mammals of past ages. During the last century and a half the discovery of fossils of giant reptiles, the dinosaurs, has overshadowed the giant mammal discoveries in popularity. But it was the mammal bones, not dinosaur bones, that became so entwined with the myths, even the myth of the reptilian dragon.

The reason is simple enough: there are more giant mammal bones in existence than there are dinosaur bones. The dinosaurs were completely extinct 70 million years ago, and many of the giant mammals survived until a mere 10,000 years ago. In the period between the extinction of the dinosaurs and the rise of the great mammals the earth underwent extensive geological changes so that a far greater proportion of fossil mammals survived than the earlier remains of dinosaurs, even though dinosaurs may have been more numerous and certainly inhabited the earth longer.

A major problem in hunting and particularly in preserving ancient mammal fossils comes from their being so recent. Older fossils have undergone chemical changes that have literally turned them to stone. Although there are fewer older fossils, they are better preserved. Many ancient mammal bones are so close to the surface that they can be exposed by rainstorms, plant roots, or burrowing animals. Once stripped of the protective layer of earth, these bones will often disintegrate rapidly if not properly cared for. Hence, the numerous stories of the giants' bones "crumbling to dust" when exposed to the air.

Despite their present fame, the existence of giant reptiles was not even recognized until the early part of the nineteenth century. Dinosaur bones probably had been found earlier, but they had not been identified properly. On July 25, 1806, William Clark, co-leader of the famous Lewis and Clark expedition, dug a large bone out of rocks on the south bank of the Yellow River below Billings, Montana. Later this site proved to be rich in dinosaur bones. Clark extracted a broken bone, the remains of which were three feet long and several inches around, yet he merely described it as "the rib of a fish."

2

The Science of Old Bones

TODAY IT IS EASY to laugh at the legends of human giants, dragons, and unicorns with which people of the past sought to explain the huge bones they found. These interpretations seem fantastic and foolish in the twentieth century, but we have to recall what the state of knowledge concerning the earth and the development of life upon it was in past centuries.

The age of the earth was not considered to be very great. In 1650 Archbishop James Ussher of Ireland collected all the age references in the Old Testament and from them calculated that the earth had been created in the year 4004 B.C. Some copies of the Bible had this date printed in the margin of the first chapter of Genesis. Later Biblical scholars fixed the time of Creation even more precisely. They declared the Creation began at nine in the morning of October 26, 4004 B.C. The idea that the Creation took exactly six days as stated in Genesis was also strongly held.

Not everybody held these views. Belief in the literal truth of the Bible was crumbling as early as the fifteenth century. Indeed, clergymen contributed many of the observations and theories that finally brought Archbishop Ussher's date and the six-day Creation crashing down.

A hundred years after Archbishop Ussher's pronouncement most people had abandoned the 4004 B.C. date, but they still did not think the earth was very old. Around 1750 the French naturalist, the Comte de Buffon, performed experiments which led him to the conclusion that the age of the earth was 74,832 years—still a very short span of time considering the current estimate that the earth is at least 4.5 billion years old.

Another strongly held belief was that all the animals on the earth had remained unchanged from the day of Creation. There could be no extinct species. If a creature had been created then it must still exist somewhere on earth. President Thomas Jefferson, a man with a keen scientific mind, expressed the belief thus: "Such is the economy of nature, that no instance can be produced of her having permitted any one race of her animals to become extinct; of her having formed any link in her great work so weak as to be broken."

These prevailing views of the earth and life upon it were challenged by the existence of fossils. There are many different kinds of fossils. Today the word has come to mean any remains or traces of creatures from past times that became buried and preserved in the rocks of the earth's crust.

People have been turning up fossils for a very long time. Prehistoric men collected fossil shells and made jewelry from them, but it is doubtful that the cave man speculated much on the origins of these stones that looked like sea shells. But in the fourth and fifth centuries B.C. the Greeks did speculate on these fossils and many of the speculators came to the conclusion that the fossils were the remains of living things.

The Greeks had been on the right track, but their wisdom was forgotten and later a very influential man considered the problem and decided there was no way that living things could turn to stone. That man was the Arabic scholar Avicenna who lived from A.D. 980 to 1037. In Avicenna's day learning in Europe was at a low ebb while scholarship flourished in Arabic lands. Avicenna himself was the most renowned scholar in the world, and his influence persisted a long time after his death, not only among the Arabs but in Europe as well.

31

Avicenna postulated some sort of natural "shaping force" which playfully changed ordinary stone into the image of living things. He called this force *vis plastica*. Avicenna's *vis plastica* was called in to explain many otherwise inexplicable fossils.

Belief in *vis plastica* did not keep men like Boccaccio from seeing the bones of giants in the fossil bones of elephants. The bones of giant mammals clearly had belonged to living creatures. The idea that the earth was once inhabited by a race of giants which had died out existed side by side with the idea that all species had remained unchanged and intact since the day of Creation and none could become extinct. Few were bothered by the contradictory nature of these beliefs.

Although fossils had been known for a long time, the word "fossil" was first coined by Georgius Agricola, a sixteenth-century physician who practiced in a mining area of his native Germany. Agricola was fascinated by mining and wrote a treatise on the subject. Mining had never been written about before, and in order to do so Agricola had to make up many new words. Mining is digging and the Latin word "to dig" is *fodere*. Agricola called miners *fosseres* and what the miners dug up, *fossilia*. Originally, *fossilia* meant anything brought to the surface, but gradually the word "fossil" came to be applied only to those strange stones which resembled living things.

Slowly, during the seventeenth century, the science of paleontology (roughly, the knowledge of things that existed a long time ago) was born. The concept that fossils had once been living things proved far easier for most people to accept than the idea that there were species on the earth which had died out.

Johann Jacob Scheuchzer (1672–1733) was one of the early scientists to recognize the nature of fossils. Yet when he was presented with a strange-looking fossil, over a yard in length and clearly showing a skull and backbone as well as a number of ribs, he declared it to be "the sad remains of a sinner who drowned in the Flood." Scheuchzer published his opinion in 1726. Fortunately, he had already died by 1811 when another scientist, the Baron Georges de Cuvier, looked at the fossil and declared, quite correctly, that this old "sinner" was in reality the fossil remains of a giant salamander. Perhaps it was with a touch of malice that Cuvier named the fossil salamander *Andrias scheuchzeri,* in memory of Scheuchzer.

Georges Léopold Chrétien Frédéric Dagobert Baron de Cuvier was a man who was every bit as imposing as his magnificently long name suggests. He was a superb anatomist, who more than anyone before him was able to understand the relationship of one part of the body to another. From a fragmentary skeleton, Cuvier was not only able to gain an accurate picture of the appearance of an unknown animal, he was also able to infer a great deal about the animal's habits.

There is a story told about Cuvier which illustrates how well he understood that the function of one part of an organism was intimately related to the function of all others. As a prank, one of Cuvier's students dressed in a devil costume, complete with horns and cloven hoofs, and entered the anatomist's bedroom while he was asleep. "Cuvier, Cuvier, I have come to eat you," the diabolically costumed student said. Cuvier opened his eyes, glanced at the "devil" sleepily and replied, "All creatures with horns and hoofs are plant eaters. You can't eat me." Then he rolled over and went back to sleep.

Cuvier was the first man to extend the classification and anatomical study of animals to fossil as well as living animals. He almost single-handedly founded the science of paleontology. During his lifetime (1769–1832), Baron Cuvier became the leading figure in biology and the virtual dictator of the biological sciences in Europe.

It is doubly unfortunate, therefore, that Cuvier had a severe scientific blind spot. He simply could not accept the idea of evolution.

Long before Charles Darwin published his epic "The Origin of

33

Species" many other men, including Darwin's own grandfather Erasmus, pondered the problem of ancient and extinct animals and had come to the conclusion that one species evolved into another. What Charles Darwin did was provide an overwhelming number of facts in support of evolution and suggest a method by which evolution was accomplished. The full title of his book outlines the method, "On the Origin of Species by Means of Natural Selection, or the Preservation of Favoured Races in the Struggle for Life."

Cuvier died before Darwin's work was published in 1859, but it is doubtful that even if he had lived to read it, he would have altered his antievolution opinions. Cuvier was a proud and stubborn man, fiercely devoted to his own theories. In order to explain the extinction of species, Cuvier had adopted the idea that the world was swept by periodic catastrophes in which large numbers of species were wiped out and others created anew. The most recent of these catastrophes, many asserted, was the Flood described in the Bible.

Cuvier did not invent the theory of catastrophism; it was an ancient idea. But his support enabled the doctrine to dominate European science. Evolutionists could make no headway against such formidable opposition.

Cuvier conducted a furious crusade against his older contemporary the Chevalier de Lamarck, the leading evolutionist before Darwin. Lamarck was not the careful scientist that Cuvier was, and the Baron not only exposed but maliciously ridiculed his rival's errors. In the end, of course, it turned out that Lamarck was much closer to the truth than Cuvier, but while the two men were alive, Cuvier had all the better of the arguments.

Today, Cuvier is remembered chiefly for his heavy-handed opposition to evolutionary ideas—a sad reputation for a man who was a great scientist. By Cuvier's time, and largely through his influence, men no longer sought to explain giant bones with tales

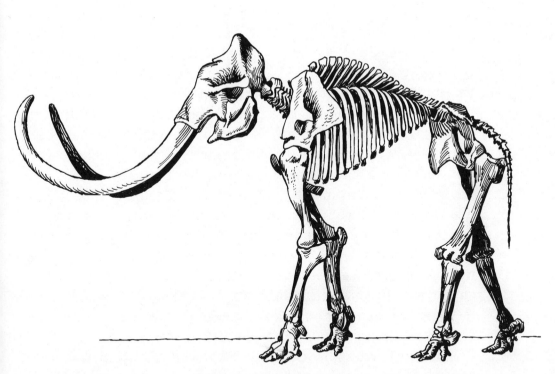

Skeleton of mammoth

of a mythical Cyclops. When Cuvier received a shipment of huge bones from South America, he correctly identified them as belonging to a gigantic relative of the little tree sloth. Cuvier supervised the assembly of these bones into a complete skeleton. When the skeleton was put on display, it created something of a sensation. The German dramatist Goethe looked at the skeleton and called it a "miraculous animal."

Naturally, not everyone accepted Cuvier's views about extinct species. When he announced the discovery of elephant and rhinoceros bones in Europe, the die-hards gravely informed him that this could not be so because elephants and rhinoceroses did not live in Europe. The bones, they asserted, were those of war elephants brought to Europe by Pyrrhus the King of Epirus who warred against Rome in the third century B.C. Other bones, particularly those of elephant-like creatures were explained away as being the remains of Hannibal's famous elephants or as in the case of those found in London in 1716, the elephants of the Roman emperor, Claudius.

The final major figure in the development of paleontology is Charles Darwin himself. Darwin's voyage around the world on the ship, *Beagle*, and his development of the theory of evolution are well known. It is interesting to point out that Darwin encountered the bones of giant mammals during his voyage, and they impressed him profoundly. South America was particularly rich in very large and very strange fossil bones. Darwin bought the skull of the extinct mammal *Toxodon* for eighteen cents. Here was an animal that had never been seen before, and one that would not fit into any of the recognized classifications. Darwin saw armadillos for the first time, and he also saw the skeletons of animals that were very much like armadillos but much, much larger.

While in South America, Darwin wrote in his journal: "The number of the remains embedded in the grand estuary deposit which forms the Pampas [in the southern part of Argentina] and covers the granitic rocks of Banda Oriental, must be extraordinarily great. I believe a straight line drawn in any direction through the Pampas would cut through some skeleton or bones . . . The origin of such names as 'the stream of the animal,' 'the hill of the giant,' is obvious . . . We may conclude that the whole area of the Pampas is one wide sepulchre of these extinct gigantic quadrupeds."

Darwin returned from his voyage to his native England in 1837 and spent the next twenty years slowly evolving his own theory of evolution. During that period he published nothing on the theory. He was not only meticulously careful, but he was also convinced that other men were as rational as he was. He knew his theory contradicted many established biological and religious ideas. His hope was that if he amassed enough facts in support of evolution, the opposition would be won over without bitterness.

Darwin was finally virtually forced into publishing his ideas when he discovered that another British naturalist, Alfred Russel Wallace, was just about to publish an almost identical theory of evolution. Darwin always felt that one of the reasons that there was such violent controversy concerning his theory was that he had "hurried" into proclaiming it before it was fully formed.

The debate which engulfed Darwin's "The Origin of Species" was a bitter one, and one in which the evidence of the bones of the giants and other fossils played an important role. Thomas Henry Huxley, one of the most vigorous champions of Darwin's ideas, exclaimed, "If the theory of evolution had not existed before, paleontology would now have to posit it."

The gigantic bones which men had so often viewed with wonder were no longer looked upon as belonging to a race of mythical giants or to Hannibal's elephants. They were studied for what they were—the gigantic relatives of animals still living today.

A glamourous pioneering era of paleontology began and scientists started turning up more gigantic fossils from all parts of the globe. So numerous were these huge animals that the Biblical statement, "There were giants in the earth in those days," seemed to be true after all.

Before we go on to examine the giant mammals that roamed the earth we have some rather dull but important business to take care of. From here on we are going to be confronted with an alarming number of long, and unfamiliar, names. It would be easier if there were some way to avoid them, some way of simplifying the technical names used by paleontologists and geologists, but there is no way out.

Once the general outlines of the classification systems are mastered the names will not present any problems. And if you forget whether the Tertiary period comes before or after the Cretaceous period, or whether an order is bigger than a class, you can always refer back to these pages.

First, we have to consider the millions of years during which the events described in this book took place. Just as we divide the year into months, weeks, and days, geologists (the scientists most concerned with the age of the earth) have divided up the 4.5 billion-year-history of our planet into units. The largest of these are called eras—there are six of them, but only the three most recent, the Cenozoic, Mesozoic and Paleozoic, concern us. It is only in these eras that the remains of living things have been found in abundance. The giant mammals themselves lived only during the Cenozoic, the most recent era, the one in which we are living. Eras are further subdivided into periods, and the periods are broken down into smaller epochs.

When dealing with geological time, it is important to remember that the divisions are not rigid. If you look at a chart with thick lines separating one period from another, you get the impression that abrupt changes took place between the periods. In most cases, there were no such sharp changes. The divisions blend smoothly into one another.

Geological classification can be compared to a historian's classification such as "the Victorian era." The era coincides roughly with the reign of Queen Victoria of England. But the name of the Queen is only a convenient label—what is being described is a whole way of life which existed at the time. No one can say exactly when the Victorian era began and when it ended. What happened is more important in determining the boundaries of the Victorian era than any dates.

Next, we need a rudimentary knowledge of biological classification. So let's start at the bottom with the smallest group, the species. A species is a single kind of animal. Individuals of a species can interbreed freely with one another. Next in the classification hierarchy is the genus, a group of closely related species. Scientists generally refer to animals by both their genus and species name. Your

GEOLOGICAL TIME

ERA	PERIOD	EPOCH	REPRESENTATIVE LIFE
CENOZOIC	QUATERNARY 0-1 million years	Recent Pleistocene	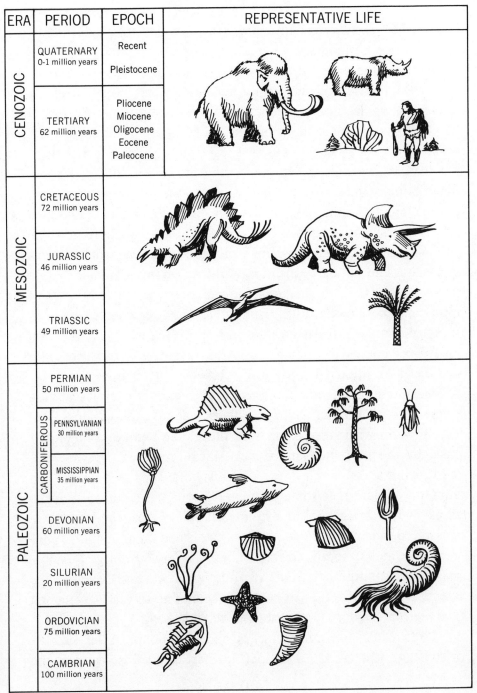
	TERTIARY 62 million years	Pliocene Miocene Oligocene Eocene Paleocene	
MESOZOIC	CRETACEOUS 72 million years		
	JURASSIC 46 million years		
	TRIASSIC 49 million years		
PALEOZOIC	PERMIAN 50 million years		
	CARBONIFEROUS — PENNSYLVANIAN 30 million years		
	CARBONIFEROUS — MISSISSIPPIAN 35 million years		
	DEVONIAN 60 million years		
	SILURIAN 20 million years		
	ORDOVICIAN 75 million years		
	CAMBRIAN 100 million years		

pet dog is *Canis familiaris*. The genus *Canis* includes wolves and jackels, but the species name *familiaris* tells you that only the domestic dog is designated.

Going up the scale, the next classification after genus is family. For the domestic dog the family is Canida. This larger grouping includes a whole variety of foxes, which are not quite as closely related to the dog as are the wolf and jackel. Next up the scale is the order, Carnivora—carnivores or meat eaters. Not only the dogs, but the cats, weasels, bears, and many others are included under this heading. One step more and we are at the class. For the dog it is Mammalia or mammals—all warm blooded animals. The next largest classification is the phylum, Chordata or chordates—all animals with backbones, which includes everything from a shark to a man. The final classification is the kingdom—animal.

That's the basic classification. In practice, there are all sorts of suborders and superfamilies. But we will not need such details.

As you can see, the names are in Latin. When the classification system became established back in the seventeenth century Latin was the international language of scholars and scientists.

The system of classification is applied to extinct as well as living animals. With extinct animals—since we have only bones and teeth to work with—the problems of putting an animal in its proper place are much greater, and the classification system is less exact.

In giving an animal a name, scientists often try to pick a Latin word which describes some characteristic of the creature. For example, when bones of an extinct relative of the elephant were discovered, scientists decided it must have been an animal of frightening size and strength, so they called it *Dinotherium* or "terrible beast." When different kinds of dinotheres were discovered, the scientists had to distinguish between them. The largest was named *Dinotherium gigantissium*—"hugest terrible beast."

At other times the animal may be named in honor of the scientist or someone who played an important part in the discovery of the animal. *Rhytina stelleri*, the giant sea cow, was named after Georg Wilhelm Steller who first described it scientifically.

A final point concerns fossils. As we have seen, there are many different kinds of fossils. The kind we are mainly concerned with in this book are fossil bones. Bones get covered by earth and over the centuries mineral-bearing waters seep into them. By a process known as *permineralization*, the organic matter is partially or completely replaced by the minerals. Thus, the fossil retains the shape, but not the chemical structure, of the original bone. A fossil bone is more durable than the original. While a bone will decay in a few years, fossil bones last for millions of years.

We can now take a look at the world as it was 70 million years ago when one tribe of giants was dying and another was about to be born.

3

A World Without Giants

THE MAMMALS began their rapid evolutionary expansion some 70 million years ago at the beginning of the era geologists call the Cenozoic, "the Age of New Life." The Mesozoic era, "the Age of Middle Life" had been the time of the rise and dominance of the reptiles, particularly the dinosaurs. Then after over 100 million years of success, dinosaurs disappeared from the land and all the rest of the ruling reptiles went with them. The *pterosaurs* and other flying reptiles disappeared from the skies. The swimming reptiles—*ichthyosaurs, mosasaurs* and *plesiosaurs*—which had dominated the Mesozoic seas also vanished. "They all went," wrote the Canadian paleontologist W. E. Swinton, "without a single survivor or descendant." None of today's reptiles can count the dinosaurs, *pterosaurs* or *plesiosaurs* among their direct ancestors. By the end of the Cretaceous, the last period of the Mesozoic era, the ruling reptiles had reached an evolutionary dead end.

Says American paleontologist Dr. Edwin H. Colbert, of the dinosaurs, "Not one of them survived into a later geologic age, as is amply proved by the fact that during almost a century and a half of paleontological exploration, the wide world over, no trace of a dinosaur bone or tooth has ever been found in any post-Cretaceous rocks, not even in the earliest of them. The proof of the geologic record on this score is irrefutable." Alas, there is no substance to the belief that dinosaurs may still live in the depths of some unexplored jungle or on some remote island.

The reasons for the extinction of the ruling reptiles pose a fascinating puzzle. Says Dr. Colbert, ". . . the problem of extinction is one to which we return, time and again, even though very little is known about it. The most hardheaded and blasé geologist is more often than not apt to get excited when he becomes involved in a discussion of the extinction of the dinosaurs."

Aside from the inherent fascination attached to the problem of the disappearance of these enormous reptiles, the extinction has a direct bearing on a discussion of giant mammals. With the dinosaurs gone, and other reptiles severely reduced in size and numbers, land and sea were left open for the development of mammalian giants. In some cases, the mammals matched in size, appearance, and way of life the reptiles which had died out ages before. Scientists say that the mammals filled the ecological niches left vacant by the extinction of the reptiles.

Another reason for spending a moment on the disappearance of the dinosaurs is that a wave of abrupt mass extinctions also occurred among the giant mammals. Is it possible that they suffered a fate similar to that of the dinosaurs?

At one time the extinction of the dinosaurs was explained by assuming that they were wiped out in some sort of natural catastrophe. Scientists no longer accept this view. "Catastrophes are the mainstays of people who have very little knowledge of the natural world; for them the invocation of catastrophes is an easy way to explain great events. But the modern student of nature is quite aware that the evolution of the earth and the evolution of life upon the earth have not proceeded by catastrophic events, even though local catastrophes—the eruption of a volcano or the sweep of an epidemic—may temporarily affect the progress of nature in some specific area," says Dr. Colbert.

During the late part of the Cretaceous—the age in which the dinosaurs were most numerous and successful—the world began experiencing what geologists call the Laramide Revolution. This was the series of earth movements which ultimately brought forth our modern mountain systems—the Himalayas, the Andes, the Alps and the Rocky Mountains. Throughout the world, land surfaces seemed to be rising. Low continental areas which had been inundated by shallow inland seas were lifted, and the shallow seas receded and dried up.

These slow but dramatic earth changes altered the world's climate and plant life. The dinosaurs of the early Cretaceous lived in a world of primitive plants, while those of the late Cretaceous lived amid the sort of plant life with which we are still familiar today.

The most commonly offered explanation for the extinction of the dinosaurs is that they could not survive the colder temperatures brought on by the earth changes, nor the changes in vegetation caused by the cold. The problem with this explanation is that many of the dinosaurs did survive these changes. The changes began to take place long before the dinosaurs died out and dinosaurs continued to flourish though the world had altered profoundly. Why didn't some of the dinosaurs, at least the smaller ones, survive longer? Why aren't they still around today? Other reptiles, like the crocodile, have continued to exist.

An odd explanation—perhaps not an entirely serious one—has been expressed by the witty German paleontologist, Fritz Kahn. He notes that the primitive forests were made up mainly of ferns. "Ferns contain purgative oils," he says, "and thus with the disappearance of the fern forests the giants lost their accustomed laxative. The great masters of the earth became depressed, indifferent about fighting and sex, and so they ingloriously died out from constipation."

But a change in vegetation does not explain the disappearance of the great reptiles from the sea. There could have been no drastic alterations in the temperature or salt content of the oceans during this time because the turtles and fishes continued virtually unaffected.

Another common assumption is that the dinosaurs died out because the world got colder, but Professor R. B. Cowles has suggested that a rise in the temperature may have brought about their demise. The temperature regulation mechanism of large reptiles like the dinosaur is not efficient, and dinosaurs could easily overheat. Overheating would either kill off the dinosaurs directly or damage the heat-sensitive reproductive cells. There are two problems with this theory. First, there is no evidence that world-wide temperatures rose at the end of the Cretaceous and, second, although increased heat might have had serious effects on large dinosaurs, it would not have such an effect on the many smaller dinosaurs.

The next theory says the dinosaurs were wiped out in a "survival of the fittest" struggle with more vigorous, more intelligent, and more adaptable mammals. The fatal flaw in this theory is that the dinosaurs were already gone before the mammals began their evolutionary explosion. Dinosaurs dominated the land for 100 million years and during that entire period, warm-blooded little mammals had also existed. Both dinosaurs and mammals had evolved at about the same time. But as long as the ruling reptiles were around, the mammals remained small, insignificant, and stagnant from an evolutionary point of view.

If the mammals did not bring about the extinction of the dinosaurs through direct competition, perhaps they brought it about by eating the dinosaurs' eggs. One of the most publicized paleontological expeditions of all times was the one headed by Roy Chapman Andrews in the Gobi desert of central Asia. Andrews brought back hundreds of dinosaur eggs. Some of these eggs bore the tooth marks of primitive mammals. But again the question arises—why were just the dinosaurs harmed? Why not other egg laying reptiles as well? And how could the mammals have harmed the great marine reptiles?

How about epidemics sweeping through the dinosaur world? Everything we know about epidemics makes this explanation unlikely. An epidemic might have destroyed a single species of dino-saur, but not all of them, and the marine and flying reptiles as well.

In recent years even astronomers have involved themselves in the discussion of the extinction of the dinosaurs. Some have sug-gested that at the end of the Cretaceous, the earth was bombarded by an unusually heavy concentration of cosmic rays. This could have been caused either by a supernova—the sudden flare up of a star—somewhere within the vicinity of our solar system, or by a weakening of the earth's magnetic field.

Recent investigations indicate that the magnetic field which sur-rounds the earth does weaken periodically. When it does, much of the earth's protection from cosmic rays disappears. We know that radiation can affect reproductive cells. A cosmic ray bombardment could have had a disastrous effect on the dinosaurs and other large reptiles. The tiny mammals which may have lived in holes in the ground would have been less affected by the bombardment. But radiation is not selective. Why would all the dinosaurs have been affected while other reptiles like the crocodiles and the turtles re-mained untouched? The cosmic ray theory sounds rather like the old catastrophe theories set down in the language of the space age. Fascinating as the problem of the extinction of the dinosaurs is, we have no final answers at present.

Although the extinction of the dinosaurs was rapid—geologically speaking—it took many, many years. The species probably died out one or two at a time. If a man had been alive at the end of the Cretaceous he might not have been aware that the dinosaurs were a dying race. Only a tiny percentage of the vast tribe would disap-pear during the span of a single human lifetime.

Is there something really odd about the disappearance of the dinosaurs? Some scientists think not. Writes Fritz Kahn, "There has been much discussion about the causes of the rise and fall of the saurians (dinosaurs). But why? Are not two hundred million years enough for the dominance of a family, and a hundred million years for the despotism of giants? Is not Olympus vacant now and the Parthenon a ruin? Why do we expect any stock to be immortal? Everyone knows that everything mortal is mortal . . . Families die out; so do nations, races, and so too have the saurians disappeared. It only seems rapid to us because it lies so far back in the past and because in a hundred million years, one can toss ten million around as if they were nothing."

Whatever the reasons, at the end of the Cretaceous—70 million years ago—the earth was wiped clean of the giant reptiles. The mammals started their rise to dominance in a world that had been depopulated of large animals. The earth was ready for a new race of giants—warm-blooded giants.

4

Early Mammal Giants

IT IS IMPORTANT to remember that tiny mammals existed throughout the age of dinosaurs, but that they become successful only after, and probably because, the dinosaurs died out.

Fairly early in the evolutionary history of the reptiles, in the late Pennsylvanian age, a subclass of reptiles, synapsids or mammal-like reptiles, branched off from the line of reptilian evolution that led to the dinosaurs and to modern reptiles. During the next 100 million years the synapsids had evolved into undoubted mammals. Just when and where the line between mammal and reptile was crossed we cannot determine.

It is an academic problem in any case. Today the differences between mammals and reptiles seem clear. Reptiles lay eggs; mammals bear their young alive. The body temperature of a reptile varies greatly; mammals maintain a consistent body temperature (this is what is meant by "warm-blooded"). Mammals are covered with hair, while reptiles have a scaly exterior. But even today the lines are sometimes blurred. Primitive mammals of the monotreme family, the duckbill platypus and the anteaters, *Echidna* and *Tachyglossus*, lay eggs, yet have all the other characteristics of true mammals. The word mammal comes from *mammae*, or milk glands. The monotremes have milk glands but of an extremely primitive nature; they are little more than modified sweat glands.

The problem of drawing the line between mammal and reptile is almost an impossible job for the paleontologist who has only bones

48

to work with, and sometimes not even a complete skeleton. The ictidosaurs which developed during the Triassic period have skeletons that display a striking mixture of mammalian and reptilian characteristics. They are usually classed as advanced reptiles, but we have no way of knowing whether they were covered with hair, had a consistent body temperature, or bore their young alive.

Fossils of the first creatures that paleontologists can unhesitatingly class as mammals appear in rocks from Jurassic times. Fairly early in the history of mammals four distinct orders can be discerned.

There were no giants among the earliest mammals. On the contrary, most were tiny—about the size of mice—although one, the *Triconodon*, reached the size of a house cat. The mammal-like reptiles had all been carnivorous and three of the four known orders of

Cynognathus, a mammal-like reptile

49

Jurassic mammals had teeth which indicated that they too were meat eaters, or more probably insect eaters. The fourth order, the Multituberculates, seem to have been the first herbivorous mammals. Of the four orders of early mammals, only that group known as the Pantotheres had any real evolutionary future. All of today's mammals, with the possible exception of the small number of monotremes, are descended from the Pantotheres.

About the end of the Jurassic, the Pantotheres split along two major evolutionary lines, the marsupials and the placentals. Both groups are still represented in the world. The name "marsupial" comes from the Latin word meaning "pouch." Marsupial young are born in an extremely undeveloped state. Many marsupials have a pouch in which the young can be protected after birth until they are able to lead an independent life. The kangaroo is the best known marsupial, but the opossum has the greatest range and is the most successful marsupial living today. Practically all mammals today, except the opossum and those from Australia, are placental mammals.

In placental mammals, the embryo takes longer to develop and the young are born at a more advanced stage. Therefore, they are able to take up an independent existence more quickly than the young of the marsupials. This is the major difference between the marsupials and the placentals.

Because their method of reproduction seems more primitive, marsupials are often viewed as a stage in the development from egg-laying reptile to placental mammal. In truth, both marsupials and placentals seem to have developed at about the same time from the same sort of egg-laying ancestor.

During the long reign of the dinosaurs the marsupials and placentals shared the small number of ecological niches allocated to mammals. But with the end of dinosaur dominance there was a great evolutionary spurt by the placentals. The number of marsupials also increased, but they did not match the expansion among

A typical early mammal compared to the skeleton of the foot of
the dinosaur *Tyrannosaurus*

the placentals. A number of factors may have given placental mammals an advantage. The advanced state of development of the young should have insured a higher survival rate. Placentals also seem to have possessed larger brains and therefore superior intelligence.

In most parts of the world the marsupials were either exterminated or held to an insignificant position as compared with that of the rapidly proliferating placental mammals.

Only in two areas were the marsupials able to compete successfully. At the end of Cretaceous times, Australia became separated from the other continents. This was before the evolutionary spurt of the placentals and Australian marsupials had little competition. They evolved into a vast array of different species and have continued as the dominant mammals of Australia to the present day.

Somewhat after Australia became isolated, South America too became isolated from the rest of the land masses of the world. In

South America, the marsupials had to compete only with primitive placentals. The more advanced and successful placentals that were evolving in other parts of the world had no opportunity to move in. For some 60 million years, South America was a haven for marsupials. But then, at the end of the Tertiary period, the land bridge between South and North America rose and a host of advanced placental immigrants from the north swept down onto the southern continent and displaced most of the distinctive marsupial species that had developed there. These northern invaders were a mixed lot—everything from pigs to cats.

While marsupials have generally remained small, a few giants did develop among them. Indeed, today's red kangaroo, which can grow to a height of over seven feet, and weigh two hundred pounds is almost a modern giant. Fossils of kangaroos that stood ten to twelve feet tall have been found in Australia. These giant kangaroos must have been able to make fantastic leaps. A modern kangaroo can jump twenty-five feet from a dead stop and, when going at full speed, can cover forty or more feet in one bound. The bones of the giant kangaroos indicate that they had stronger legs than those found in modern types.

A giant opossum six feet long has been found, but the real giant among fossil marsupials is another Australian specimen, *Diprotodon*. In life it probably resembled the bear-like Australian marsupial, the wombat. *Diprotodon* reached a length of twelve feet. This was small compared to some of the real giants that evolved among the placentals.

The first mammal giants developed among the plant-eating ungulates or hoofed mammals. (The name "ungulates" is not a particularly descriptive one, for while some ungulates have well developed hoofs, others have claws.) A giant of its time was *Phenacodus*, a creature with a cat-like body and pig-like head. The name means "deceiver toothed" because the teeth do not seem to go with the rest of the body. Although technically a hoofed mammal, *Phenac-*

Phenacodus

odus had well-developed claws. Its eating habits must have been as unspecialized as its appearance. To paleontologists the teeth look suitable for either a plant-eating or flesh-eating way of life. It is probable that *Phenacodus* would eat almost anything. The largest known species was about the size of a large pig—not a true giant yet, but on the way.

Even larger creatures were developing among that ungulate group paleontologists have labeled amblypods, or "blunt footed." One of this group called *Sparactolambda* was a good-sized creature with a hideous appearance. Instead of hoofs, it possessed large well-developed claws, and its teeth were long and fang-like. *Sparactolambda's* habits, however, were peaceful. Both teeth and claws seem to have been designed for digging up roots rather than tearing flesh.

Barylambda, standing four feet high and eight feet long, may well have been the largest animal of the early Cenozoic. This curious creature was weighted heavily toward the rear, with a long thick tail and massive back legs. The front legs were shorter, and the head was small and blunt. Like all mammals of this early period, *Barylambda's* little skull had only a tiny amount of space allotted for the brain.

A close relative of *Barylambda* was *Coryphodon*. The fossil remains of this animal are numerous, suggesting that in its time it was quite successful. *Coryphodon* may have resembled a small hippopotamus, with one notable exception. *Coryphodon* had wicked-looking sharp incisors protruding from its mouth. The name is derived from these teeth, for *Coryphodon* means "pointed tooth."

Barylambda was eclipsed in size by a beast that might have stepped right out of a nightmare—*Uintatherium*. The name comes

Coryphodon

from the Uintas Mountains in Utah where fossils of the creature were first located.

Uintatherium looks like no other animal living or dead. Its appearance is so bizarre that when first discovered, some scientists assumed it was a kind of horned dinosaur. Only after more extensive remains were found could they be sure that the animal was a mammal.

Several varieties of this creature developed during the Eocene age. Although they resembled the amblypods, paleontologists have grouped them together in their own separate order with the descriptive name of Dinocerata or "terrible horned ones."

The largest of the uintatheres developed during late Eocene time. It stood seven feet high at the shoulder and had a body twelve feet long. The massive bones suggest that *Uintatherium* was as thick and heavy as an elephant. But any resemblance ended at the head. The largest uintathere had a skull forty inches long. Projecting from the skull were three pairs of blunt, bony horns. The largest of these three pairs of horns was some twelve inches. Nine-inch-long fangs curved downward from the creature's upper jaw. Its lower jaw was equipped with flanges to protect the fangs from breakage.

For all its bulk, *Uintatherium* had an exceptionally small brain case. The animal was larger than the modern rhinoceros, but its brain was smaller, and the rhino is not known as a brainy animal. *Uintatherium* must have been a dull-witted beast. But this seemed to be no disadvantage in the world of early Eocene times, for the uintatheres continued to grow and flourish for a period of nearly 20 million years.

Few fossil discoveries have created as much excitement as the discovery of the uintatheres. The excitement was not only due to the creature's weird appearance or its unique place in evolutionary history. Fossils from the order Dinocerata were discovered almost simultaneously by two of the bitterest rivals in scientific history, Edward Drinker Cope and Othniel Charles Marsh. The two men were more than professional rivals; they had developed a deep personal hatred of one another.

Cope and Marsh were America's leading paleontologists during the nineteenth century. They were the first scientists to do any extensive digging in the western United States, which contains some of the world's finest fossil deposits.

Early in the 1870's, Marsh made some important discoveries and his reputation was on the rise. Then Cope uncovered the first of his Dinocerata fossils. The animal was strange looking enough, but Cope's initial reconstruction made it look even stranger. In addition to the six horns and saber-like teeth, Cope gave his creature a long trunk, like an elephant. He called his find *Eobasileus* or "dawn emperor" and said it was the most unusual fossil ever discovered in America. This was a direct slap at Marsh who had made similar claims for some of his own discoveries.

Soon afterward Cope came upon the remains of a somewhat similar creature. But on the basis of this new find, he was forced to revise his original reconstruction. Cope was frantic now, for he knew that Marsh and his staff were conducting excavations nearby. He feared that Marsh would discover the same kind of fossil and then use his powerful scientific connections to claim priority of discovery.

The discoverer of a new species has the right to give it a name. Naming a creature, then having that name accepted by fellow scientists, is almost a sacred act among paleontologists. Cope made it a practice to use the newly installed telegraph lines to transmit his scientific names back to the East, so that Marsh could not rush in with his own name first. In this case the telegraph proved to be Cope's undoing. For his old *Eobasileus*, Cope picked the name *Loxolophodon* which described the animal's strange slanting teeth. But the long Latin word was too much for the telegraph operators. When Cope's telegram arrived in the East the name had been so garbled that no one knew what to make of it.

56

Uintatherium

As Cope had feared, Marsh also discovered fossils of the same strange creature. No less advanced than Cope, Marsh also rushed to the telegraph office. He called his fossil *Dinoceras*, "terror horn." It was an easier name, but it still was garbled in transmission to *Tinoceras*. But at least the scientists in the East could make something out of Marsh's name, and it was accepted.

Marsh too was confused by the animal's appearance. He asserted that the saber-like tusks of his *Dinoceras* were used in exactly the same manner as the great teeth of the saber-toothed cat—that *Dinoceras* was a carnivore. It was a revolutionary idea and a wrong one. Scientists now believe that the tusks were used for cutting water plants upon which the creatures fed.

The Dinocerata evolved in North America and then migrated to Asia. Representatives of the order have been found in the Gobi desert. Both American and Asian species died out during the early Tertiary. Perhaps a climate change which resulted in a general drying up of the swamps of the world was the reason for their extinction.

The earliest of the mammals were probably insect eaters or insectivores. They were hardly large enough to be anything else, but the change from insect-eating habits to a truly carnivorous or flesh-eating mode of life is a minor step. As the plant-eating mammals grew in size, the flesh-eating mammals they preyed upon also grew. None of the carnivores reached the size of *Uintatherium*, but one well-known species, *Patriofelis*, did grow as large as a modern lion.

The name *Patriofelis* is misleading because it means "father cat," and the creature was not directly related to cats. It was a creodont, the earliest class of truly carnivorous mammals. The word means "flesh toothed" and refers to the teeth of these animals that were adapted for cutting and tearing meat.

Patriofelis was a massive, and doubtless clumsy, animal of Eocene times. Certain features about it—notably a large thick tail—indicate that *Patriofelis* may have been adapted for a partly aquatic life. The tail would have been a powerful paddle useful in propelling *Patriofelis'* bulky form through the water.

Creodonts evolved along several different lines. Some apparently were not strictly flesh eaters; they may have been carrion eaters, rather like the modern hyena. Others like the European *Arctocyan* and the American *Claendon* rivaled bears in size and, like bears, could eat a wide range of foods.

The real giant among the creodonts was *Andrewsarchus*, represented by a single skull found in Mongolia. The skull was three feet long. If the rest of the animal was proportioned like a typical creodont, it had a body twelve feet long.

The creodonts, like the amblypods and other plant-eaters that they hunted, had small brains. Unlike today's carnivores—cats, dogs, weasels, and the like—the creodonts were not built for speed or agility. They were fit only to hunt the slower moving animals of the day.

Creodonts, amblypods, and their contemporaries are called archaic fauna. They began developing in Paleocene times, the earliest age of the Cenozoic, and dominated the earth through the Eocene epoch, and then gradually died out. The archaic fauna ultimately went to extinction without a surviving descendant. They seem to have lost the struggle for survival with the mammals that developed during Eocene times. These new mammals were more intelligent, faster, and more adaptable. They became the ancestors of the mammals of the future, including most of those alive today.

5

South American Giants

FOR SOME 60 million years—the period called Tertiary by geologists—South America was isolated from the rest of the world. North America, Asia, Europe, and Africa were all joined in what might be called the World Continent. Europe and Asia are today really a single continental land mass. There is a land connection between the Eurasian continent and Africa. At the Bering Strait in the northern Pacific, the North American continent is only a few miles from Asia, and during most of the Age of Mammals, the two continents were connected.

But while North and South America are now joined by the narrow Isthmus of Panama, they were separated by a fairly large area of water for millions of years. The isolation allowed South America to evolve its own highly unique and often gigantic animals.

Australia too was isolated, for an even longer period, but that continent seems to have produced few giants. In any case, the fossil history of Australian mammals is very poorly known.

In earliest Tertiary times, the primitive and relatively unspecialized mammals that inhabited most of the world also inhabited South America. Then the land bridge between South America and the rest of the world sank. Often the creatures that evolved in South America paralleled or converged with those which had evolved in the World Continent. Parallel evolution is the development of similar characteristics in related but geographically isolated animals. Convergent evolution is the development of similar characteristics in unrelated animals. Dramatic examples of both types of evolution occurred in South America.

For reasons that evolutionists have not been able to explain, most of the early South American carnivores, or meat eaters, came from marsupial stock. A good example of convergent evolution was *Borhyaena*—not a giant, but an undoubtedly fierce beast about the size of a small wolf. In fact, *Borhyaena's* skeleton indicates that it was very wolf-like in appearance. An even more striking example of convergent evolution was *Thylacosmilus*. This was an animal about the size of a modern tiger. It had a short cat-like skull and tremendously long fangs. On its lower jaw was a deep flange of bone which protected the fangs when the creature had its mouth closed. Although *Thylacosmilus* was a marsupial, its resemblance to the famous saber-toothed cats that evolved in North America is truly astonishing.

One group of placental mammals that reached its highest peak of evolution in South America was unique and did not resemble anything else in the world. These were the edentates. The word means "without teeth," but the literal translation is misleading. Many of the edentates do have teeth. But all of them are adapted to diets where the teeth, if not completely unnecessary, are rather small and unimportant. The armadillo, tree sloth, and anteater are modern edentates. They do not constitute an important group today. But in Tertiary times there were edentates of gigantic size.

The modern armadillo is a heavily armored creature with solid shields of bone over the shoulders and hips. The shields are connected by flexible bands of horny material so that the armadillo does not have a rigid back like a turtle. But the armadillo has light weight armor compared to the glyptodonts, giant cousins of armadillos. The glyptodonts had a solid bony shell covering their backs. The skeleton of a glyptodont bears a remarkable, although superficial, resemblance to the skeleton of a great turtle.

Not only was the glyptodont's back protected, it also had a bony

Comparison of *Thylacosmilus*, a South American carnivorous marsupial (left), and *Smilodon*, largest of the saber-toothed cats

"helmet" to protect its head. Nor was the tail left exposed; it was encased in rings of armor. In some species the tail ended in a large spiked knob of bone, that looked like the mace used by medieval knights and undoubtedly served the same purpose. With this spiked tail the glyptodont could deliver a deadly blow to an enemy.

There were several varieties of glyptodonts, the largest being *Glyptodon*—fourteen feet long and five and one-half feet from its foot to the highest point on the dome of its body armor.

To support the weight of all of their armor, glyptodonts had unusually heavy skeletons. The back legs were particularly massive and the animal would have been capable of walking for short distances on its hind legs as modern armadillos occasionally do. The front legs were not as well developed, but often bore large claws.

Such claws could have been used for digging out roots, but they could also have been formidable weapons in a fight. It is difficult to imagine how any carnivore could successfully attack one of these armored giants.

About one million years ago, when the land bridge between North and South America again rose from the sea, the main flow of migration was from the North to the South. But a few of the old South American types not only withstood the influx of newcomers, but actually moved northward. The armored glyptodont was one of these. Glyptodonts became common from Argentina to Florida and survived into very nearly modern times.

A much larger edentate was the giant ground sloth. The closest living relative of the ground sloths are the tree sloths—small, sleepy creatures that spend their lives hanging upside down from the limbs of trees. The ground sloths which began evolving in South America during early Tertiary times quickly displayed a tendency to develop to a great size. The largest of them, *Megatherium*, or "great beast," was comparable to an elephant in size. It could rear up on its hind legs to a height of twenty feet.

Megatherium and the other ground sloths had thick tails and massive hind legs. These features have given rise to the belief that the ground sloth spent much of its time sitting or squatting in a semi-erect position. Thus seated, the sloth could eat the leaves off the trees. The creature's simple teeth are modified for grinding, another indication of a leafy diet.

The sloth's front feet were powerful and tipped with great curved claws. In the larger species, the claws would have been convenient hooks for pulling down branches to mouth level. In smaller sloths they could have been used for digging up roots. For any sloth, the claws could serve as wicked weapons.

Well-preserved remains of the ground sloth have been found, so we know that its body was covered with long coarse hair. The ground sloth did not have any armor like the glyptodonts, but its

Most of the world's land masses are either directly connected or were connected in the recent past. The major exception is (1) Australia. While small mammals could be carried on driftwood and bats could fly from island to island, large mammals could not. The result was that Australia had its own

giant mammals, mostly of marsupial stock. (2) A land bridge at the Bering Strait, connecting Asia and North America, existed until a few thousand years ago. (3) There was a direct land connection between North and South America some sixty million years ago. This was submerged until fairly recent times. The isolation allowed South America to develop unique giants.

skin was studded with something like a cobble-stone pavement of little bones or ossicles. These gave the ground sloth a hide tough enough to discourage the hungriest carnivore. Even the great saber-toothed cat would have been no match for a full grown *Megatherium*.

The structure of the sloth's feet indicate that these giants must have had a most ungainly walk. They shuffled along on the sides of their feet. The outside toes on the ground sloth's back feet disap-

Giant sloth

Toxodon

peared entirely and the inside ones were elongated. A thick pad on
the side of the foot bore most of the weight in walking. Like their
living relatives, the tree sloths, they probably also used their front
claws as an aid in walking.

Despite the protection offered by huge size, bony hide, and massive claws, this ponderous, clumsy creature looks so overspecialized
that it seems a perfect candidate for quick extinction. The tiny brain
case of these giants shows that they were far from the brightest crea-

The mammals of South America one million years ago

tures alive. Yet when the land bridge to North America reopened, the sloths shuffled and lumbered their way northward along with the armored glyptodonts. Ground sloths became established from Patagonia in the southern part of South America to the Great Lakes and from the Atlantic to the Pacific Oceans.

There is a genuine mystery attached to the time of the ground sloth's final extinction. It is generally assumed that they died out during Pleistocene times when so many other giant mammals also became extinct. But in the 1890's, a large piece of animal hide was discovered in southern Argentina, which many believe to have come from a medium-sized species of ground sloth known as *Mylodon*.

The best scientific estimate is still that all the ground sloths became extinct at least 10,000 years ago. But, if this fresh looking piece of hide had come from a ground sloth, then there was the possibility that the ground sloth was still alive within the last two hundred years.

Supporting this possibility were some Indian legends and stories told by early Spanish settlers of Patagonia about encounters with a huge hairy beast which could have been a ground sloth. Unfortunately, aside from the piece of hide, there was no solid evidence to lend credibility to these accounts. Stories of encounters with huge and unknown animals have come regularly from remote areas of the world. Only rarely have they described an encounter with a genuinely unknown animal.

The source of the strange piece of hide was found to be a large cave in the extreme southern part of Argentina. Scientific investigation of the cave has indicated that sloths did once inhabit it. But Carbon-14 dating of the most recent sloth remains give them a date of 10,500 years ago, well within the bounds of the conventional time given for the extinction of the sloth. None of the investigations cleared up the mystery of the apparent freshness of the sloth hide discovered in the 1890's. The mystery remains today and in the years since the hide was discovered no new light has been shed on it.

While the edentates are almost unique to South America (some early fossil edentates have been found in North America and the edentate, pangolin, still lives in Africa and Asia), the ungulates or hoofed mammals evolved into a great number of species on the World Continent as well as South America. All descended from the same basic stock, but South American isolation gave rise to some peculiar ungulate giants.

A group of South American hoofed mammals that flourished some 30 million years ago was the toxodonts. Early specimens were the size of sheep. Later ones were bulky monsters five or six feet high at the shoulder, with a body as massive as that of a rhinoceros. It was a skull of one of the later toxodonts that so impressed the young naturalist Charles Darwin when he came to South America.

A few of the toxodonts possessed rhinoceros-like horns, but most had blocky, hornless faces. They have been described as resembling "a giant guinea pig." The toxodonts seem to have been peaceful giants. Their teeth indicate that they were primarily browsers and grazers. One of the largest types had widely spaced protruding upper teeth which gave it a humorous, buck-toothed look.

Many of the small relatives of the toxodonts died out after the influx of northern mammals. But the giant toxodonts stood up well in the face of this migration. They survived until the mass extinctions of the Pleistocene.

If the toxodonts paralleled the rhinoceros, *Macrauchenia* paralleled the camel in size and general structure. The name *Macrauchenia* means "great neck." One interesting feature is that in some species the nasal opening of the skull is far back on the face. This has led paleontologists to assume that *Macrauchenia* had a flexible proboscis or short trunk. *Macrauchenia* was another survivor of the northern invasion. It lived until Pleistocene times.

Two South American giants which seem, at least in superficial ways, to parallel the elephants were *Astrapotherium* and *Pyro-*

therium. Both were heavily built creatures and the construction of their skulls hint that they may have possessed some sort of trunk. Neither were very numerous and both types seem to have lost out in competition with northern mammals. At least they disappear from the fossil record after the invasion of northern mammals.

The geographical isolation of South America still provided the Age of Mammals with its share of giants, including two of the most unusual and most successful giant mammals ever to have lived— the glyptodont and the ground sloth.

6

Plant-eating Giants

IN 1911 BRITISH SCIENTISTS discovered some pieces of bone
from an enormous skeleton. The discovery was made in what
is now West Pakistan. At that time the area was known as Baluchistan. The bones were those of a mammal, and it appeared as though
the beast they had come from was of unsurpassed size in the kingdom of the mammals. But the material was too scanty to hazard a
guess as to what manner of creature it might have been.

The rumors of this incredible beast were known to the members of the American Museum of Natural History expedition of
1921–24. This was the most elaborate and successful of all fossil-
hunting expeditions. For two years the large well-equipped and
well-financed group conducted excavations throughout central
Asia. Central Asia was unexplored territory for paleontologists.
The expedition which was headed by Roy Chapman Andrews was
looking primarily for bones of man's ancestors. They did not find
any; instead, they found dinosaur eggs, and on August 5, 1922, in
the Tsagn-Nor basin of Mongolia members of the expedition dug
up more bones of the Asian giant mammal.

What they found were 365 bone fragments. These were sent
back to the American Museum in New York for cleaning and assembly. All the fragments seemed to come from the animal's skull.
But that would make the skull so enormous that Henry Fairfield
Osborn, the museum's chief paleontologist, first believed that his
associates in the field had made a mistake and had really sent him

bone fragments from several skulls. No mistake had been made. All 365 pieces belonged to one skull—a skull that was four and a half feet long. At that, the giant's head proved to be small in comparison to its body.

The Asian giant has been given the name *Baluchitherium*—"the beast from Baluchistan." Additional finds have given us a more complete picture of this giant. *Baluchitherium* stood seventeen feet high at the shoulder and with its long neck it could have nibbled at branches twenty-two feet above the ground. It was sixteen feet long and fairly bulky in build. Estimates of weight are hazardous, but the creature probably weighed between ten and twenty tons.

Baluchitherium's teeth and mouth indicate that it was a browser. It had only two front teeth, which were probably used for nipping buds and twigs. In addition to the usual grinding teeth, *Baluchitherium* possessed a thick pad of cartilage in the front of its jaw which probably served as a platform against which coarse, tough food was crushed.

How many of these giants lived is unknown. Fossils of the creature are rare. Indeed, no complete skeleton has ever been found. This may either be because the animal was not very numerous or because it lived under conditions which made preservation difficult. Equally unknown is the length of time these giants walked the earth. Their fossils come from rocks laid down in Asia during Miocene times, 20 million years ago.

Most authorities believe that *Baluchitherium* was the largest land mammal that ever lived. Of course, no one can be sure, but in the more than half century since it was first discovered no animal has been found that rivals it in size. For a variety of reasons it would seem as though land mammals much larger than *Baluchitherium* would face almost insurmountable problems of feeding and locomotion. But we should not be too hasty in such a judgment. We have to remember that while *Baluchitherium* may have weighed twenty tons, the largest of the dinosaurs was able to drag a fifty-ton

Baluchitherium, the largest land mammal

body around. And dinosaurs exceeding twenty tons were rather common creatures of the land.

Paleontologists were quickly able to classify *Baluchitherium* as a relative of the modern rhinoceros by its teeth. The giant lacked the characteristic horn on its nose, and must have relied entirely on its great size to protect it from attack.

Today the rhinoceros family has been reduced to a few closely related species. These are so rare that the entire family is dangerously close to total extinction. But throughout much of the Age of Mammals they were common.

Teleoceras was a long, heavy bodied rhinoceros of Miocene times. It often grew to a length of eleven feet. The odd thing about *Teleoceras* was that its legs seemed much too short for its body. From an anatomical point of view, *Teleoceras* was a misshapen beast and one unfit for survival. But in Miocene times the short legs were apparently no disadvantage, for the abundance of fossil remains indicate that *Teleoceras* was common in North America.

The name *Teleoceras* means "end horn." The traditional picture of a rhinoceros is of a creature with a large horn on the end of its nose. The name rhinoceros means "nose horn." But as we have already seen, *Baluchitherium* was a hornless "nose horn," and there were many others. It is difficult for paleontologists to decide which of the rhinoceroses had horns and which did not. The horn of the rhinoceros is unique. It is made up entirely of coalesced hair and is rarely fossilized. The presence of a horn is usually indicated by a roughened area on the skull where the horn was attached. *Teleoceras* must have had a fairly short horn, perhaps little more than a knob protruding through the skin.

The modern rhinoceros, like the modern elephant, is exclusively a resident of warm climates. But during the Ice Age the woolly rhinoceros was one of the most common creatures living on the cold fringes of the glaciers. In most ways the woolly rhinoceros resembled modern forms. The difference is that it was covered by

74

a thick coat of hair, while today's rhinos are nearly hairless. We know a good deal about the appearance of the woolly rhinoceros because of a particularly fortunate find in Poland. There a completely preserved woolly rhinoceros carcass was found in soil saturated with oil. The oil preserved the flesh and hair of the animal. Confirming evidence for the woolly rhinoceros' appearance comes from cave drawings. This creature was a favorite subject for prehistoric artists, and doubtless for prehistoric hunters as well.

The rhinoceros and their kin are ungulates, mammals with hoofs. Scientists divide the hoofed mammals into two groups—the perisso-

Woolly rhinoceros

dactyls, those which usually have an odd number of toes, and artiodactyls, which usually have an even number of toes. (Hoof, by the
way, simply means the horny covering that protects the end of an
animal's toe. In a horse this has evolved into a single massive covering. Deer have two hoofs, but for many other animals the hoof
does not cover the entire foot.) Giantism was most common among
the perissodactyls.

The titanotheres or "gigantic beasts" are the best known of the
extinct perissodactyl giants. The oldest titanothere fossils come
from early Eocene times. They were small animals then, about the
size of a large dog. But fossils indicate a remarkably rapid increase
in size. By middle Oligocene times there were gigantic titanotheres,
some seven feet high at the shoulder and fifteen feet long. They
were built like a rhinoceros, but bigger, and probably equaled elephants in weight.

The first of the titanotheres to be discovered by paleontologists
was actually one of the last to evolve. This was Othniel Charles
Marsh's *Brontotherium* or "thunder beast," named after the creature in the mythology of the Sioux Indians. *Brontotherium's* nose
ended in an enormous saddle-shaped horn. (Strictly speaking, the
titanothere's impressive skull adornments were not true horns, but
they can be called that for the sake of convenience.)

The development of the titanothere's horn has been the subject
of a lot of debate among evolutionists. Early titanotheres had no
horns at all, while 20 million years later (a very short time from an
evolutionary point of view) they possessed the massive saddle-
shaped protuberances. Paleontologists have been able to trace the
development of the horns from a simple thickening of the bone in
the nose region, through small, seemingly useless, horns to the
great horn of *Brontotherium* itself.

How and why did these horns develop? The American paleontologist George Gaylord Simpson has proposed this theory:

"It is likely that the animals had the habit of butting each other

Brontotherium

and their enemies, even at this stage [among the early hornless titanotheres]; they had already become rather stocky, lumbering creatures with stout heads, and they had no other evident means of fighting. Thickening of the bones in the butting region would then be of advantage. The claim that the thickening was not enough to be useful at all or to be effective in orienting further change is not valid in the light of present knowledge. Any thickening would be of some advantage, however slight this might be, and many studies have now shown that in populations of medium to great abundance any appreciable advantage, even though exceedingly slight, may be surprisingly effective in producing further change of the same sort in subsequent generations."

For many years scientists believed that the titanotheres were a group that developed and lived exclusively in North America. But fairly recent finds indicate that in late Eocene and early Oligocene times they pushed into Asia, and even made their way as far as Eastern Europe.

The fossil record for titanotheres is quite good. We can see how in a short time they evolved from a small nonspecialized hoofed mammal into a family of giants that contained a large number of successful and widespread species. Then, as speedily as they appeared, they disappeared and not a single descendant of the once numerous titanotheres survives. What happened? Looking into the mouths of these giants, paleontologists speculate that they succumbed to dental problems. The titanotheres' teeth were not highly developed and seemingly did not keep pace with their evolution in size.

As long as the world's vegetation remained soft, the titanotheres could grind up enough food with their primitive teeth. But as the world's vegetation changed and hard grasses replaced soft plants, the giants' teeth could not stand the strain. They simply wore out on the tough vegetation, and doomed the titanotheres to starvation.

Closely related to the titanotheres was the group known as

chalicotheres. The largest member of this group (a creature about the size of a modern horse) puzzled paleontologists for many years. This anatomical oddity has been given the name *Moropus* or "foolish-footed" because instead of hoofs its feet bore three large, stout claws. The rest of the skeleton seemed to place *Moropus* among the perissodactyls, but the claws confused the identification. When the first skeletons were found, scientists thought they had the bones of two different animals mixed up. Only after numerous finds did the paleontologists finally become convinced that despite its clawed feet *Moropus* really was one animal.

Moropus

79

Moropus was a plant eater, and the claws were used either to dig up roots or pull down branches. Whatever the claws were used for, the chalicotheres got on well enough in their own peculiar way. They were never numerous, but one form or another from this group seems to have been around throughout almost the entire Cenezoic era. They became extinct only during the Pleistocene.

Perissodactyls are still common in today's world. The horse is undoubtedly the most familiar. But during Miocene times perissodactyls were the dominant hoofed mammals. In more recent times, however, they have lost their place to the artiodactyls, those hoofed mammals with an even number of toes. Here, too, the name should not be taken too literally, for one group of artiodactyls has three toes. The classification is not based only on the number of toes but rather on a whole host of characteristics.

Man owes a lot to the artiodactyls. Most of our familiar domestic animals belong to this group: sheep, cattle, goats, pigs, camels, and llamas. In addition, deer, antelopes, giraffes, bison, and one of the most successful modern giants, the hippopotamus, are also artiodactyls.

An early artiodactyl giant was *Dinohyus*—the "terrible hog." The creature was terrible in appearance, but there is some question as to whether it was a hog. Many authorities believe the relationship between *Dinohyus* and the pig family is very distant. But in any case *Dinohyus* looked like a wild pig—if you can imagine a wild pig the size of a bison. *Dinohyus* was six feet high at the shoulder and eleven feet long. Three feet of that length was skull. Add to this enormous fangs and large bony protuberances to protect the eyes, and one can easily imagine that the living *Dinohyus* presented a terrifying picture. We have no way of knowing whether it really was an aggressive and dangerous animal or a shy, peace-loving one. All we can determine is that the fangs were used for digging out the roots which made up a major part of *Dinohyus'* diet.

Dinohyus fossils are fairly common in Miocene rocks in the

Dinohyus

western United States, particularly Nebraska. After Miocene times, however, *Dinohyus* and his kind became extinct. Perhaps they lost the struggle for survival with the wild pigs that began migrating to North America and probably competed with *Dinohyus* for edible roots. Although *Dinohyus* had an outsized skull, the area for the brain case remained small. *Dinohyus* must have been an unintelligent giant. Pigs, on the other hand, are considered extremely intelligent and adaptable animals.

The pigs themselves started small and over the centuries showed a tendency toward a moderate increase in size. No true giants ever developed among them until modern times when monsters of a ton or more have been produced by selective breeding among domestic pigs.

Today, the camel is virtually the symbol of the deserts of Asia and North Africa. Yet, like the horse, the camel originally evolved on the North American continent, then migrated to Asia. And like the horse, the camel died out in North America at the end of the Pleistocene, but managed to survive in Asia.

During the evolution of the camel there were many side branches. One was the so-called "giraffe camels." The giant of the camels belongs to this group; it is named *Alticamelus*—"high camel." The name was well deserved, for *Alticamelus* stood eighteen feet tall. It was a thin, long-legged, long-necked creature that probably used its great height to eat the leaves from trees just as the modern giraffe does.

The large family of deer and deer-like creatures has produced few giants. All the evolutionary energy of the deer family seems to have been concentrated on growing an exotic variety of horns. There were deer with four horns, and deer with six horns, deer with horns on the top of their heads, and deer with horns on the ends of their noses. And then there was a deer with horns so large that it must be considered a giant. This was the Irish elk.

The popular name, Irish elk, is unusually misleading, for the animal is not exclusively Irish and is not a true elk. The scientific name *Megaceros*, meaning "great-horned," is more appropriate. *Megaceros* stood six feet at the shoulder, but what was truly gigantic about it were its antlers which had a spread of up to ten feet and weighed eighty pounds. *Megaceros* had the largest antlers of any known deer.

Antlers are rarely preserved as fossils, but most *Megaceros* skeletons have been found in European and, particularly, Irish bogs. Bogs are unusually well suited for preserving biological specimens, so a large number of antlers have survived and practically every large museum in the United States has a set on display.

The antlers of the Irish elk are so enormous that some scientists believe they must have become a distinct disadvantage. "Some per-

Alticamelus compared with modern camel

sons feel that the weight of the antlers overbalanced *Megaceros* when it leaned forward to drink," says William E. Scheele of the Cleveland Museum of Natural History. "Since so many of the known skeletons have come from bogs, it is assumed that once an animal of this size fell into such a bog it could not escape and eventually died there."

George Gaylord Simpson has pointed out that *Megaceros*, like other deer, shed its antlers and had to regrow a new pair every year. "It seems that yearly replacement of these masses of bone must have been a severe physiological burden and that the strain of carrying such a weight on the head must also have been severe."

Megaceros or Irish elk

Megaceros was not a particularly successful animal, for it survived for only a few thousand years, becoming extinct during the late Pleistocene. According to Simpson, "There is a total lack of decisive evidence that this development [the antlers] did, in fact, cause the extinction of the group, but it does seem possible that it was a factor in that extinction."

We do know that during the Pleistocene epoch, man hunted *Megaceros*, and many implements have been found that were fashioned from the bones or antlers of this animal. The size and weight of a ten-foot spread of antlers would have been a great handicap for a hunted animal and they would have been poor defensive weapons against human hunters.

Why did *Megaceros* develop those enormous antlers which seem not only useless, but downright hazardous to the animal's survival? Such a development looks like a direct contradiction to the evolutionary principle of survival of the fittest. It may have been an evolutionary quirk, says Simpson. Deer of *Megaceros'* type "have a growth pattern in which as the body size becomes bigger the antlers become even bigger; they increase not only in absolute size but also in size relative to the body of the animal. In such a group, if there was an evolutionary trend toward larger adult body size, there would also, automatically, be a trend toward relatively larger antlers. The Irish elk had the largest body of any deer in this group, and its antlers are just the size to be expected if the inherited relative growth pattern remained the same."

With a height of eighteen feet the giraffe is the tallest living animal. But the spindly legs and tremendously elongated neck are fairly recent developments. The earliest creatures on the line leading to giraffes are found in rocks from Miocene times. They seem to have evolved from primitive types of deer, and thus are not very large. But the modern giraffe can count a few giants among its ancestors.

For centuries the people in the vicinity of the Siwalik hills of

Long-horned bison

northern India had been digging up large bones. Naturally, the bones were attributed to human giants. In the 1830's scientists began to take an interest in these bones, and when they investigated the source they found some of the best fossil deposits in Asia. Among the many remains discovered in the Siwalik hills were those of *Sivatherium giganteum*, a large heavy-bodied relative of the giraffe. On its head *Sivatherium* had two huge flaring horns between its ears, and a pair of smaller conical horns above its eyes. Variations of the *Sivatherium* type have also been found in Africa.

Sivatherium lived well into Pleistocene times and there is a possibility that this giant was still alive when man first began to organize civilization. Paleontologist Edwin H. Colbert examined an odd-looking little bronze figure made by the Sumerians, the first civilized people. The figure dates from around 3500 B.C. Archaeologists identified the figure as that of a stag, but to paleontologist

86

Colbert the stocky body and unusual arrangement of horns made it look more like *Sivatherium* than any stag.

Did *Sivatherium* survive into Sumerian times? It certainly is not impossible. The little bronze figure raises another intriguing possibility. A rope runs from the animal's muzzle, suggesting that whatever it was, it had been captured and perhaps domesticated.

Of all the artiodactyls—that large and bewilderingly varied order—a group known as the bovoids is the most numerous today. The group includes sheep, goats, antelopes, and cattle. The bison of North America deserves special mention. Before the white man settled the West, the bison was the most numerous large mammal of North America. There were an estimated 50 million bison at the beginning of the last century. The huge herds soon fell victim to the rifle and the bison was brought to the point of extinction. But during the Pleistocene there were many different kinds of bison in North America. The modern bison is the smallest known species. It probably represents a dwarfed descendant of one of the larger species of Pleistocene times. The abundance of remains indicates that the extinct species may have been as numerous as the modern bison once was. Of the closely related species of extinct bison, one stands out; *Bison priscus*, with horns that measured six feet from tip to tip.

7

The Elephants and Their Allies

WHEN WE THINK about giant animals, the elephant immediately comes to mind. Elephants are the largest land animals alive today. They are a common sight in zoos and circuses, and elephant herds still roam parts of Africa and Asia. But there are only two varieties of elephant in the modern world. This represents only a tiny remnant of a vast and varied clan of giants that once roamed much of the earth's surface.

Elephants belong to the order Proboscidea, a name taken from the marvelously active trunk which is the most distinctive feature of modern elephants. But, in their long and complex evolutionary history, not all elephants had trunks.

The British author Rudyard Kipling once wrote a story about how the elephant got his trunk. A long time ago, said Kipling, the elephant didn't have a trunk. "He had only a blackish, bulgy nose, as big as a boot, that he could wiggle about from side to side; but couldn't pick up things with." Kipling said that one day a young elephant went down to the riverside where a crocodile grabbed his nose and pulled and pulled until it was stretched out into a trunk. The story is, of course, an imaginative fable but, as it happens, the earliest elephant did not have a trunk but probably had a nose much like that described by Kipling.

The first proboscidean yet discovered flourished in Eocene times, at least 40 million years ago. The creature is named *Moeritherium*, after an ancient lake in Egypt near which its remains were found.

Superficially, *Moeritherium* resembled a pig or small hippopotamus. It stood only two feet tall at the shoulder and the structure of the skull indicates that it lacked the distinctive trunk. But, to the paleontologist, the creature's elephant-like teeth are the clue to its place in evolutionary history. *Moeritherium* was either a direct ancestor of the later proboscideans or looked very much like that ancestor.

The ancient lake region in Egypt also yielded up two other primitive proboscideans. They are *Phiomia*, "the lake province one," and *Palaeomastodon*, "the ancient mastodon." Both were true giants rivaling the modern African elephant in size. Paleontologists are undecided as to whether either of these proboscideans

Palaeomastodon

89

actually had a proboscis, or trunk. We do know that these creatures had tusks, four of them; two projecting from the upper jaw and two from the lower. Both *Phiomia* and *Palaeomastodon* displayed another evolutionary trend that was to develop to spectacular proportions in later times; their lower jaws were elongated.

The earliest elephant fossils have been found in Africa, indicating that the proboscideans began their evolution there. But they soon spread to Asia and across the then dry Bering Strait to North America and ultimately to South America. Proboscideans were among the most successful large mammals. They evolved into an enormous variety of strikingly different species, most of them gigantic. For the sake of convenience they can be divided into four categories: (1) the dinotheres; (2) the long-jawed mastodons; (3) the short-jawed or "true" mastodons; and (4) the elephants and their near ancestors and relations.

The dinotheres or "terrible beasts" are a side branch of proboscidean evolution. They were indeed giants. The smallest dinothere was a full eight feet at the shoulder and the largest stood ten feet.

The dinotheres had bulky elephant-like bodies and probably a long trunk as well. But, instead of having tusks curving out of the upper jaw, like any proper elephant, they had two tusks curved downward from the lower jaw and hooked back toward the body.

These tusks are the sort of anatomical feature that give paleontologists sleepless nights. No one has yet been able to come up with a satisfactory explanation of what use the dinotheres made of their tusks. During the last century, before a full *Dinotherium* skeleton was available, one scientist looked at the skull and decided the creature lived in the water and used the tusks for anchoring itself to the bank when it wanted to take a nap. Others believed that an aquatic dinothere used the tusks to pull itself along the ground when it ventured on to dry land. But during the last three-quarters of a century enough skeletal remains have been found to prove that

Dinotherium

the dinotheres were land animals. And still no one has been able to explain the tusks.

Could they have been used for digging up roots? It seems unlikely, for then the creature would have had to drop down onto its knees to feed—an uncomfortable and dangerous position. Perhaps the tusks served as hooks for pulling down branches? Possible, but unlikely, because the branches would have been pulled under the animal's mouth and out of reach. As weapons, the tusks look ineffective. *Dinotherium* could not have lifted his head high enough to stab any other creature. Another suggestion is that the tusks were used for scraping bark off trees for food. This is not impossible, but the tusks do not look as though they would serve this purpose very well. We have to admit that there is as yet no really satisfactory explanation for the dinotheres' strange, curving tusks.

The oldest dinothere fossils were found embedded in rocks that are 35 million years old. Whatever those strange tusks were used for, they must have served their purpose extraordinarily well, for during the next 30 million years the dinotheres grew in size, but in other respects they changed hardly at all. The history of the dinotheres is considered an outstanding example of evolutionary stability.

The dinotheres ranged widely throughout Africa, Asia, and Europe, but they never seem to have penetrated as far as North America. By the end of the Pliocene they had died out in Europe and Asia, but in Africa they held on until well into the Pleistocene.

While the dinotheres represent an offshoot in proboscidean evolution, the mastodons flowered into a wide and exotic variety of creatures. The word "mastodon," by the way, does not come from "massive" but means "breast tooth." When the tooth of a mastodon was first shown to Baron Cuvier, the great French paleontologist coined the term because he saw a resemblance between the paired mounds on the animal's molars and a woman's breasts.

The trend toward longer, lower jaws that was evident in the early proboscideans, *Phiomia* and *Palaeomastodon*, accelerated among the long-jawed mastodons. Fairly typical of this group was *Trilophodon*. The bizarre-looking giant had an exceptionally wide range. Its remains have been found throughout Europe, Asia, and Africa and some particularly fine specimens have been dug up in the western United States. *Trilophodon's* lower jaw was greatly elongated. The animal also possessed two fairly short pointed tusks

Trilophodon

much like those of the modern Asian elephant. A short trunk probably projected somewhat beyond the lower jaw. *Trilophodon* was about ten feet long. Creatures of this type roamed the forests of the world for 20 million years, from the lower Miocene until upper Pliocene times.

An even more curious looking group of mastodons are those with the descriptive name of the "shovel tuskers." Here, the mastodon's lower jaw reached its greatest size. In one species the lower jaw was an incredible seven feet long. In another, the huge deep jaw ended in two flattened tusks nearly four feet long. This jaw looks like a gigantic scoop, and that's probably how it was used. The "shovel tuskers" must have lived a semiaquatic existence and used their jaws for shoveling up water plants. A strong trunk probably hung down over the long jaw. Water plants could be gripped by the trunk and then pushed back along the lower jaw into the mouth. This seems a tedious and ineffective method of feeding, but it had its advantages, for remains of a number of highly successful species of shovel tuskers have been found in places as far distant as Nebraska and Mongolia.

Another curiosity among the mastodon clan was the rhynchorostrines, or beak-snouted mastodons, of North America. Instead of their lower jaws stretching outward, they curved down. To some, this resembled the curving beak of a bird of prey; hence the name.

The mastodon *Cordillerion* had long, spirally twisted tusks. *Anacus* was fairly small for a mastodon, being a mere eight feet at the shoulder. But it carried in front of itself a pair of remarkably long, remarkably straight tusks. These tusks often reached a length equal to two-thirds of the animal's entire body.

The true mastodons are typified by the American mastodon. From its teeth, paleontologists have been able to determine that the American mastodon was a forest dweller. The skeletons of forest-dwelling animals are not often preserved as fossils because, under forest conditions, remains decay too quickly. Yet fossil bones of the American mastodon are so common, particularly in the eastern part of the United States, that we may assume that the American mastodon once roamed the continent in enormous numbers. Some authorities feel that the herds of mastodons must have far outnumbered the herds of bison found on the Great Plains before the coming of the white man.

Fossils of over 100 individual mastodons have been recovered from one Kentucky site alone, and practically every American natural history museum has local records of mastodon finds in its vicinity. Mastodon skeletons have been found in bogs where the water has preserved some of the soft parts of the animal as well as the bones. From these extensive remains we have a good idea of what the American mastodon looked like.

It was not quite as tall as the modern African elephant. A living American mastodon would have averaged ten feet at the shoulder and about fifteen feet from the base of the tusks to the drop of the tail. Although in most respects it resembled modern elephants, its body was even more massive.

A major difference between the American mastodon and the modern elephants lay in the structure of the head. The mastodon carried its head horizontally, while in modern elephants the arrangement of the head is more vertical. Mastodons had a low, sloping brow and a long, well-developed trunk. Enormous curving tusks, sometimes nine feet in length, protruded from the American mastodon's upper jaw. Bits of skin that have been found show that the mastodon had a fairly thick coat of reddish-brown hair.

Mastodons lived in North America during the Pleistocene era, and radio-carbon dating of their remains indicate that some of them were still alive a mere 9,000 years ago. Thus, they almost certainly came into contact with the early men in America. But so far we have no tangible evidence that a face-to-face meeting ever took place. Writes William E. Scheele of the Cleveland Museum of Natural History:

95

"There is controversy over whether man and mastodons ever came into direct contact. Scattered evidence would indicate that they did, for it is difficult to believe that any animal so numerous that lived so late in our history, could have escaped some contact with early man.

"Climate, however, may have had something to do with keeping such meetings infrequent, for the early hunters may have been held in check by the cold of the north country. The boggy terrain favored by these animals may also have been too dangerous or too full of insects for man's liking."

Scientists distinguish the "true" elephants—that is, those closely related to the surviving elephants—from all the other members of the order Proboscidea by their teeth. "To the layman," writes the naturalist Richard Carrington, "the natural scientist's preoccupation with the teeth of the animals he studies often seems to be evidence of a dreary, if not actually warped, mentality. Are there not enough beautiful and interesting things about animals, he asks, that one must be forever looking into their mouths? Unfortunately, for those interested in evolution, there is no alternative to this apparently uninspiring procedure, for the teeth of living things are the surest guide to their relationships, and the way they have developed."

Bearing this in mind, we can understand why the first of the true elephants is called *Stegodon*, the "roof-toothed one." The name comes from the molars which bear fourteen roof-like ridges on their surface. The earliest *Stegodon* remains come from Pliocene rocks in Asia. Somewhat later remains have been found in Africa.

Two lines of evolutionary descent branched off from the basic *Stegodon* stock. One led to the present-day African elephants, the other to the Asian or Indian elephants.

Among the primitive relatives of the African elephants was one of the largest of the proboscidean clan, *Palaeoloxodon antiquus*. This creature was distinguished by its great size—some individuals

American mastodon

reached a height of fourteen feet at the shoulder—and by its great straight tusks which jutted out of its upper jaw like a pair of enormous swords. *Palaeoloxodon antiquus* flourished in Europe and north Africa during the Pleistocene period, and then, like so many other giants, it suddenly became extinct.

Most of the other relatives of the African elephant so far discovered are fairly small, the largest being just a bit over six feet at the shoulder.

The ancestry of the Asian elephant is imperfectly known. But somewhere on the evolutionary line that led to these elephants the mammoths branched off. Of all the giant mammals of past ages the mammoth is best known to us, for its remains have been preserved in a most extraordinary way.

The mammoth was not named for its teeth. The name is a corruption of a Russian word, *mammout*. Mammoth bones and tusks were commonly found in Siberia. It has been estimated that over the years the Russians sold the tusks of at least 45,000 mammoths on the world ivory markets. But Siberia contained more than mammoth tusks and bones. Occasionally a complete carcass of one of these ancient elephants has been dug out of the permafrost, or permanently frozen ground, of Siberia.

The great abundance of mammoth bones and the occasional preserved carcass naturally gave rise to a large number of legends among the people of Siberia. The most persistent one was that the mammoth was really some sort of gigantic creature that lived underground and appeared on the surface only rarely. When it did appear the sunlight immediately struck it dead, which explained why no one had ever seen a living mammoth. The mammoth was identified with the Biblical behemoth. Legends said that the creature had been brought to Siberia from the Holy Land by Arab travelers.

There are at least four distinct and different types of mammoths. The two most famous are *Mammuthus imperator*, the imperial

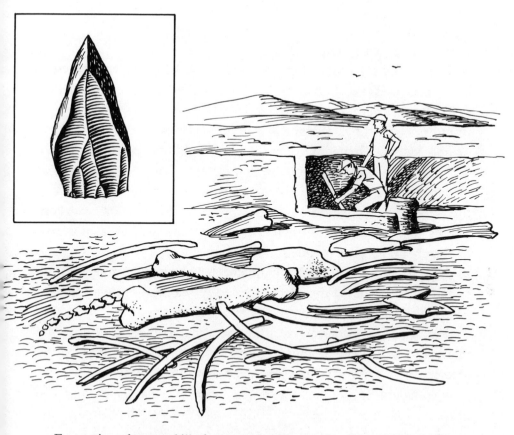

Excavation of a mass kill of mammoths. Spear point (inset) found amid
bones proves mammoths were killed by man.

mammoth, and *Mammuthus primigenius*, commonly known as the
wooly mammoth. The scientific name of the woolly mammoth means
first-born mammoth. Although it was the last of the mammoths to
evolve, it was the first to be identified.

The imperial mammoth may well have been the largest elephant
that ever lived. Skeletons have been found that measure fifteen feet
at the shoulder. The imperial mammoth evolved in Asia and migrated to North America during Pleistocene times. Tremendous
herds of these enormous beasts once roamed the southern Great
Plains. We also know that early man in North America hunted

99

mammoths, because flint arrowheads and spear points have been found mixed with mammoth bones.

The woolly mammoth is even more famous because of the complete carcasses that have been found embedded in the Siberian permafrost. There has been a good deal of needless mystery surrounding the discovery of the frozen mammoths. Many people have wondered how "tropical" animals like elephants got so far north. The answer is that the woolly mammoth was not a tropical animal at all. It was an animal of the Ice Age and lived on the fringes of the great glaciers which covered large parts of the northern continents. As the glaciers advanced, the mammoth herds migrated before them. As they receded, the mammoths followed the ice back to the north. Thus, at one time or another during the repeated advance and retreat of the glaciers, woolly mammoths lived over a vast area of Europe, Asia, and North America.

We should not be surprised that an animal as large as the woolly mammoth was able to find enough to eat on the fringes of the glaciers. The tundra vegetation of cold climates looks sparse, but it is sufficient to support large plant-eating animals today. The musk ox and the reindeer are both large animals which live in the far north and have diets similar to that of the woolly mammoth of Pleistocene times.

The frozen carcasses have shown that the mammoths possessed a thick coat of hair to protect them from the severe weather. The woolly mammoth's teeth also differed from those of its near relatives. They were harder and contained more ridges, making them exceptionally effective grinding instruments. This specialization was necessary for chewing the coarse tundra vegetation.

Many have wondered how these ancient beasts came to be frozen. Again, much of the mystery is based on misconception. The woolly mammoths became embedded in the permafrost anywhere from 10,000 to 25,000 years ago. This is a very long time ago, to be sure, but it is not all that long ago, geologically speaking.

Woolly mammoth and cave drawings of mammoths

Secondly, the finds of frozen mammoths have not been as numerous, nor have the carcasses been as well preserved, as many of the stories indicate.

Theories of catastrophic extinctions die hard. Many who still seek catastrophes to explain evolution point to the frozen mammoths as evidence. They say that enormous numbers of these animals were overwhelmed in a catastrophe and then quick-frozen during a drastic change in climate. The facts, however, simply do not support this dramatic picture.

It is impossible to say how each of the frozen mammoths met its end, but in at least one case, the remains were well preserved enough to allow scientists to attempt a reconstruction of what happened.

The Beresovka mammoth found in Siberia in 1901 is the most perfectly preserved mammoth specimen ever found. Scientists believe this animal died as the result of a fall into a deep crevice. The fall shattered the animal's pelvis and one foot and caused internal injuries. The creature may have tried to pull its great bulk out of the crevice, but failed. After a few hours it died of its injuries. Temperatures within the crevice were sufficiently low to keep the body from rotting. Mud and dirt from the surface covered the carcass and froze, encasing the entire elephant in the permafrost—ground that never thaws. Thousands of years later the carcass was partially exposed by a landslide.

This particular mammoth was so well preserved that the remains of its last meal could be found in its stomach and embedded between the ridges of its teeth. All the plants eaten by the Beresovka mammoth still grow in the Beresovka area today. This clearly indicates that there has been no catastrophic change in climate from the time of the mammoth's death to our own.

The woolly mammoth was not as large as some of the modern elephants; it averaged only twelve feet in height at the shoulder. This is about the size of the Asian elephant but smaller than the

African elephant. However, with its high domed forehead and thick coat of hair, the woolly mammoth looked larger than it really was.

In the woolly mammoth the tusks reached their apex of development. One woolly mammoth tusk measuring sixteen feet, five inches in length, is nearly half again as large as the largest tusk from a modern elephant. Mammoth tusks grew differently from those of the modern elephants. They curved outward and then back toward one another. Sometimes the tips actually crossed. This unusual development has led to a good deal of speculation concerning how the tusks were used. It has generally been assumed that an elephant's tusks were primarily weapons. This is how living elephants employ their tusks. But the enormous curved tusks of the woolly mammoth with their points turned inward would not have been very good weapons. Some authorities have theorized that the tusks circled around to serve as sort of a bumper to protect the delicate trunk, but the idea seems farfetched.

The most probable explanation is that the really enormous curved tusks served no function at all, but merely represented an overdevelopment that occurred among older mammoths. While these individuals were young and their tusks still growing, they would have been straighter and served as excellent stabbing weapons. Thus, the mammoth would have had full use of its tusks while it was in its breeding prime. But the tusks kept growing and mammoths long past their prime would have tusks that had become useless ivory circles.

During the nineteenth century, man had accepted the idea that extinct creatures, including extinct varieties of elephants, had once existed. But since most people believed that the world was swept by periodic catastrophes that wiped out all life, they could not believe that man and mammoth had lived at the same time. The coexistence of man and mammoth was proved conclusively when ancient drawings of woolly mammoths were discovered on the walls of caves in Spain and France.

Scientists believe that the Stone Age hunters made these draw-ings as part of a magical ritual before going out to hunt. The magician would draw a picture of the mammoth or other animal the hunters of the tribe wished to kill. Often these drawings show the animal pierced with spears or caught in a trap. The hunters obviously hoped that the scene in the picture would be re-enacted during the hunt.

Before leaving the mammoths, one final question must be an-swered. Are mammoths really extinct, or do a few hardy survivors still roam the unexplored regions of the Arctic? From time to time

Arsinoitherium

stories appear in newspapers and magazines which hint that a mammoth has been found alive. Unfortunately, every one of these stories has turned out to be either the result of a misunderstanding or a deliberate hoax.

A particularly persuasive story about the killing of the last surviving mammoth was widely circulated at the end of the last century. According to the story, the remains of the mammoth had been given to the Smithsonian Institution in Washington. Many people went to the Smithsonian to see the remains, and the officials there found it extremely difficult to convince visitors that the Smithsonian did not possess the skin of a freshly killed mammoth.

There is one more curious giant that is usually lumped in with the elephants, mainly because no one is sure just where else to classify it. This is *Arsinoitherium*. It was thus named because the first remains were found in Egypt near the ruined palace of the ancient queen, Arsinoe.

Arsinoitherium has some features in common with the order Proboscidea, but at best it is a distant relative. The animal's ancestors are unknown, and it does not seem to have left any descendants. It has attained a position of splendid isolation, an order all of its own—the Embrythopoda or "heavy footed ones."

Arsinoitherium lived during Oligocene times, 35 to 40 million years ago. It was a heavy bodied animal which stood five and one-half feet high and was eleven feet long. *Arsinoitherium's* most striking feature was a pair of enormous horns which grew out of its nasal bones. This made it look somewhat like a double-horned rhinoceros. Actually, *Arsinoitherium* had four horns. A much smaller pair rose straight up behind the main horns. The large horns were so massive that they had to be supported by an extra bar of bone that ran from the base of the horns between the nostrils and was attached to the upper jawbone. Perhaps someday paleontologists will make discoveries that will reveal more of the history and fate of this mysteriously isolated giant.

8

Carnivorous Giants
and Giant Apes

MEAT-EATING ANIMALS do not get as large as plant-eating animals. One of the largest land carnivores was the dinosaur *Tyrannosaurus rex*, which measured some fifty feet from nose to tail and stood twenty feet tall. But the largest of the plant-eating dinosaurs were twice that size, and outweighed *Tyrannosaurus* many times.

A really enormous carnivore would soon eat up all its available food supply. Then, too, a carnivore must hunt and kill its prey. It has to be more active and agile than the animals it hunts and great size is not compatible with great speed and agility. The problem is even more acute among mammals than it was among the dinosaurs, for a quick-moving carnivorous mammal requires more food per pound of body weight than the less active reptile.

But still, there are a number of creatures that evolved among the carnivorous mammals that can quite properly be classed as giants of their kind.

The most striking of the large carnivores of the past are the so-called saber-toothed tigers. This popular name is thoroughly misleading. The saber-toothed "tiger," or rather the group of saber-toothed cats, for there were many members of the cat family that had greatly elongated fangs, is not closely related to the tigers or to any other modern cat. Cats can be divided into two groups—the stabbing cats or saber-toothed forms, now extinct, and the biting cats, the class in which all modern cats are included.

Among the large numbers of saber-toothed cats that evolved during the 35 million years or so that they walked the earth, the largest was *Smilodon*. The name means "carving knife tooth," and it is an appropriate description of the thick, pointed nine-inch fangs, or canine teeth, which protruded from the animal's upper jaw. *Smilodon* was a little shorter than the modern lion, but considerably more massive in build.

Modern cats depend on their speed and agility as well as their tremendous strength to bring down their prey. But the heavily built *Smilodon* probably relied more on brute power and the stabbing effectiveness of its fangs.

When *Smilodon* hunted in North America the continent was populated with mammoths, giant sloths, and other large but slow-moving herbivores. Such creatures could not run; their protection was their size and the thickness of their hides. *Smilodon* with its powerful body and huge fangs would have been a deadly antagonist for young or disabled ground sloths and mammoths.

Smilodon was superbly equipped for death struggles with large animals. Its short muscular legs and heavily muscled shoulders would allow it to cling to its prey. *Smilodon's* neck and jaws were also heavily muscled so that it had the power to slash and stab with its fangs. Perhaps the jaws possessed enough power to pierce even the bone-studded hide of the adult giant sloth. *Smilodon* could open its mouth very wide so that the lower jaw would not interfere with the stabbing action of the fangs. Even its nose was pushed back so that it could continue to breathe while hanging on to its prey, waiting for the victim to bleed to death. Slow-moving as it may have been, compared to modern cats, the plant-eating giants of the time were slower still.

Paleontologists have spent a good deal of time studying the teeth of the saber-toothed cats. These teeth present a puzzle. No one has been able to figure out exactly how *Smilodon* or others of its kind could chew with such teeth. Some authorities believe *Smilodon* slashed chunks of its victims' flesh with its fangs and then swallowed them whole. Others think *Smilodon* lived exclusively on blood licked from the wounds inflicted by the saber-like fangs.

People have often looked at the enormous fangs of *Smilodon* and come to the conclusion that it became extinct because the fangs got too long and it could no longer bite effectively. Says paleontologist George Gaylord Simpson, "The poor sabertooth has come to figure as a horrible example, a pathetic case history of evolution gone wrong." He continues, "Now like so many things that everyone seems to know, this is not true. Sabertooths appear in the record in the early Oligocene, more or less 35,000,000 years ago, and they became extinct only yesterday, around the end of the Pleistocene . . . The fact is that during this long span of the saber-tooths they did not show a trend toward increase in relative size of the canine tooth. The fact is that the earliest sabertooth known (*Eusmilus*) had relatively one of the largest canines known in the group. Throughout their history the size of sabertooth canines varied considerably from one group to another but varied about a constant average size . . . The biting mechanism in the last saber-tooths was still perfectly effective, no less and probably no more so than in the Oligocene. To characterize as finally ineffective a mechanism that persisted without essential change in a group as abundant and obviously highly successful for some 35,000,000 years seems quaintly illogical!"

While *Smilodon* fed on giant sloths and mammoths, an even larger predator was pursuing deer, antelopes, and other fast-moving game across North America. This was *Felis atrox*, "fierce cat." *Felis atrox* might be called a giant jaguar because it was more like the jaguar than any other living species.

As far as we can determine, *Felis atrox* was relatively rare, at least compared with the saber-toothed cats. The most famous fossil deposits in the United States are those of the tar pits of Rancho La Brea in California. These deposits of sticky tar were a death trap

Smilodon

for large numbers of Pleistocene animals. They have yielded the skeletons of hundreds of saber-toothed cats but relatively few *Felis atrox* remains. The reason might be that there never were many of these giant carnivores, but there is another possible explanation. An animal would get stuck in the treacherous tar of the La Brea pits. Its struggles would attract the attention of nearby predators. Saber-toothed cats, which were accustomed to attacking slow-moving or stationary prey, would appear first. Soon they too would be trapped by the sticky tar. But *Felis atrox*, which was accustomed to bringing down running animals, might have been wary of attacking any animal stuck in the tar. The remains of these giants have come most often from caves or high rocky places. From such vantage points *Felis atrox* could have looked down upon the grazing herds below and picked its victim with care.

If the tar pits at Rancho La Brea are any true indication of the animal population of Pleistocene North America, then the most numerous carnivore was the dire wolf. The pits have yielded the remains of 1,646 individuals of this species, far more than of any other single species of animal. The probable explanation is that the dire wolf was more of a scavenger than a hunter. The dead and dying animals in the tar pits would have brought wolves by the hundreds. In most respects the dire wolf was exactly like modern wolves, but it was somewhat larger and considerably heavier.

Of all the carnivores the bears made their appearance on the scene last. They began branching off from large dog-like creatures in early Pliocene times, and reached a high point of their evolutionary history with the great cave bears of the Pleistocene. Today, bears are the largest of living land carnivores, but their Ice Age ancestors were just as large and much more common. Specimens have been found that are ten to twelve feet long and stood five feet high at the shoulder.

In popular pictures of life during the Ice Age, the cave bear is seen as a fierce predator and deadly antagonist of the cave man. In truth, however, the cave bear was mainly a vegetarian, although it had evolved from carnivorous ancestors. Even today's bears are not exclusively carnivorous. Many of them depend heavily on nuts and berries as well as insects as staple items of food. The carcasses of several cave bears have been found, preserved in Alpine caves under layers of bat droppings. The contents of the bears' stomachs were mainly vegetable matter. A large number of cave bear skulls show a particular deformation of the jaw. This is the result of a disease called *actinomycosis*, which attacks only plant eaters.

Although we have no indication that the cave bear was dangerous to man, we do know that man was dangerous to the cave bear.

Neanderthal man burying cave bear skulls

Neanderthal man, the stocky, beetle-browed subspecies of human that flourished in Europe during the Ice Age seems to have developed a religious ritual around the cave bear. In some caves large numbers of bear skulls were carefully arranged in special stone chambers. In some cases the bears' thighbones were thrust through cavities in the skull. The significance of this ritual burial of cave bear skulls is unknown, but it does prove that Neanderthal man had the strength, intelligence, and weapons to kill these shaggy giants. Many cave bear skeletons retain traces of ax blows.

The caves of Europe have provided us with a surprisingly good picture of the life of this bear. After studying the habitat of some cave bears, the French cave explorer Norbert Casteret reported:

"Clear traces have been preserved in the clay permitting us to re-construct one of the most remarkable scenes in the life of the cave bear. The bears used the natural conditions of the caves for sliding parties, the cave floor forming a great stone chute which ended in the muddy water. Many of the tracks are so clear that we even see the impress of hairs from the pelt upon the soft clay."

Because its remains are so numerous, the life of the cave bear has been studied with great thoroughness. Some scientists have come to an interesting conclusion regarding the extinction of this Ice Age giant. The Viennese zoologist Otto Antonius declared that the cave bear "domesticated itself like man."

The Ice Age was not a single period of unrelieved cold. Glaciers advanced and retreated. In many areas there were long periods during which the climate became quite mild. It was during one of these mild periods that the cave bear flourished in Europe. But the cold closed in once again. While many animals migrated as the glaciers advanced, the cave bear could not or would not. Instead, it retreated to the safety of the caves.

Of their cave existence, paleontologist Othenio Abel has this to say: "The long winter meant virtually a prison existence for two-thirds of the animal's life. It is not surprising that this prolonged internment had extremely harmful effects upon the health of the bears. Among brown bears and other large predators which are kept for many years in the confinement of cages, peculiar diseases of the spinal column develop. They are attacked by inflammations; fusing and hypertrophy of the bones appear. Almost invariably two adjacent vertebrae of the posterior thoracic and anterior lumbar region are affected by this 'prison disease.' These vertebral afflic-tions are well known from many cave bear sites."

Among cave bear remains scientists have come across an ex-traordinarily large number that come from diseased or physically degenerate individuals. Many, therefore, believe that the cave bear died from its own "self-domestication." But we cannot be sure. The idea of the degeneration of the cave bear has been questioned. The cave bear disappeared during the late Pleistocene, when so many other large mammals also became extinct. Many scientists now feel the cave bear was a victim of the same mysterious set of circumstances which brought so many other large mammals to extinction.

The pinnipeds—sea lions, walruses, and seals—are also classed among the carnivores. Some of them, like the walrus and elephant seal, can properly be called giants, but whether this group contained any giants in past ages we do not know, because few fossils have been found and scientists know very little about when or how these sea-living carnivores evolved.

The order of primates, the order to which man belongs, has remained rather small throughout its history. The earliest primates resembled the modern tree shrew, an animal about the size of a squirrel. The best evidence available today indicates that the line that led to man began with creatures very like the australopithecines, a group of small apes possessing some man-like characteristics, that evolved in southern Africa. The largest primate that we know of is the gorilla, which still exists today.

However, there is a hint—it can hardly be called more at present—that at one time there were apes of truly gigantic stature. One prominent scientist, Franz Weidenreich, has advanced the theory that man himself is descended from giant man-like apes which match the giants of the legends.

No book on giants can ignore the fascinating possibilities raised by the discovery of the teeth of the creature called *Gigantopithecus blacki*. *Gigantopithecus* means "giant ape" and *blacki* was appended by the discoverer to honor the Canadian physician and paleontologist, Davidson Black.

The story of *Gigantopithecus* began in the early 1930's in a Chinese drug store. As we have noted, the Chinese put great faith in the healing properties of "dragon bones," and such bones were standard items in Chinese drug stores. Most of the "dragon bones" were the remains of large extinct mammals.

Chinese drug stores had already led paleontologists to one extremely important fossil find. In the 1920's the source of a large number of "dragon bones" was traced to the area of Chou-K'ou Tien, in northern China, some 300 miles to the west of Peking. Among the many fossils discovered at this site were those of a primitive man the scientists called *Sinanthropus* and is popularly known as "Peking man." As it turned out, Peking man fossils were essentially identical to those discovered in the 1890's on the island of Java by Eugene Dubois, and named by the scientists *Pithecanthropus* or "ape man." The popular name for Dubois' *Pithecanthropus* is "Java man."

One of the men who had been hunting fossils in the Orient in the 1920's and '30's was the Dutch paleontologist G.H.R. von Koenigswald. He was well aware of the fossil treasures in the "dragon bones" of the Chinese druggists. In the early 1930's he was browsing through a drug store in Hong Kong when one very unusual "dragon" tooth caught his attention. The tooth was badly worn and the roots were missing, but von Koenigswald recognized the fragment that remained as belonging to an ape—an ape of gigantic proportions. This tooth was far larger than any ape tooth ever seen. Two years later a second tooth turned up in a drug store and two years after that, a third. Both these later finds were in somewhat better shape than the first.

By this time war had broken out throughout the Orient and von Koenigswald and his fossil collection disappeared in the chaos of wartime China. Before this happened, however, von Koenigswald showed the teeth to several of his associates including Franz Weidenreich. Weidenreich made casts of the three teeth and other material that von Koenigswald had acquired.

When the war was over, Weidenreich re-examined the casts and came to a startling conclusion. The teeth, he said, belonged not to a giant ape but to a giant man, "and should, therefore have been named *Gigantanthropus* [giant man] and not *Gigantopithecus* [giant ape]."

Weidenreich believed that the three teeth could be related to a puzzling fragment of a jawbone that von Koenigswald had found in Java. The jawbone was extremely large and heavy when compared to the jaw of modern man or to the jaw of any fossil man discovered to that time. Von Koenigswald had given the creature which had once owned this jaw the name *Meganthropus*. But the molars of the Chinese giant were one-third larger than those of *Meganthropus*, the Java giant.

"When we speak of giants," Weidenreich wrote, "everybody wants to know how tall they were, compared to modern man. This is an easily understandable but a very ticklish question, for there are no scales which permit us to read the stature of the body from the size of the teeth. Relatively small animals may have large teeth and vice versa. But, in most cases and especially in primates, large teeth necessitate large jaws, and large jaws a large body . . . the molars of the Chinese giant are, in volume, from five to six times larger than those of modern man . . . it may not be too far from the truth if we suggest the Java giant was much bigger than any living gorilla, and that the Chinese giant was correspondingly bigger than the Java giant—that is, one and a half times as large as the Java giant, and twice as large as a male gorilla." A full grown male gorilla weighs about 500 pounds. On the basis of Weidenreich's figures others have estimated that the Chinese giant would have been anywhere from eight to fifteen feet tall.

Weidenreich came to a sensational conclusion. "I believe that all these [giant] forms have to be ranged in the human line and that the human line leads to giants, the farther back it is traced. In other words the giants may be directly ancestral to man."

Weidenreich presented his theories to his scientific colleagues in 1945. Despite his careful arguments and excellent scientific reputation, he found almost no supporters for the giant theory. Now, a quarter of a century later, his theory still has virtually no supporters.

Since Weidenreich presented his theory Chinese scientists have reported finding three lower jaws of *Gigantopithecus*. These were taken from a cave in a high cliff in Kwangsi province. On the basis of these jaws the Chinese state that *Gigantopithecus* was definitely an ape. They say it was less human-like than the chimpanzee. Size estimates are still tricky, but the Chinese believe that *Gigantopithecus* was no larger than a large gorilla. Moreover, the Chinese say that *Gigantopithecus* lived in the early Pleistocene, and thus was too recent to be a direct ancestor of man.

9

Giants of the Air and Sea

S O FAR we have discussed only land mammals because it is on land that the mammals have been most important and most numerous. Mammals never really took to the air in great numbers. The only true flying mammals belong to the order Chiroptera—the bats. Bats are fascinating creatures, but small ones. The largest bat, the Indian fruit bat or flying fox, has a wingspread of five feet. Admittedly, a bat with a five-foot wingspread makes an impressive sight, but it cannot be considered a giant. There is nothing in the meager fossil record to suggest that bats were ever any larger than they are today. Other aerial mammals like the flying squirrel do not really fly; they glide.

Flying imposes strict size limitations on an animal. The heavier it is, the larger the wings it needs, and the more muscle it must have to power these wings. A flying animal will soon reach a point where it is too heavy to fly. Birds are marvels of lightweight construction. Size must be sacrificed to the demands of overcoming gravity.

There have been, and still are, giants in the bird family; the ostrich is a living representative. The extinct ostrich-like elephant bird from Madagascar was even larger, reaching a height of ten feet. Other ostrich-like giants were the moas which once inhabited New Zealand. All these birds had one thing in common: they could not fly. It is only because they were released from the restrictions of flight that they were able to attain great size.

Scientists estimate that the limit of an animal's flying weight is

117

somewhere between forty and fifty pounds. The only living bird that approaches the limit is the South African bustard or paauw, a goose-like bird, which can weigh nearly forty pounds. The bustard has a wingspread of nine feet. It is not known for graceful flight.

A secondary problem for potential flying giants is that flying takes a lot of energy, and consequently requires a lot of food. A giant of the air would have trouble finding enough to eat.

The prize for the largest flying animal must go to *Pteranodon*, a flying reptile with a wingspread of twenty-seven feet that lived during Jurassic times. This giant of the air was a delicately constructed creature and probably weighed no more than twenty-five pounds. But the aerodynamic facts of life make such mythological creatures as flying horses and dragons impossible.

While the air lowers the size limit on animals as compared to land, water does the opposite. Water helps support weight, and a sea animal has the potential of growing far larger than a land animal. It is not surprising that the largest mammals—indeed, the largest animals of any kind that have ever lived—are sea dwellers. These are the Cetaceans—the whales.

Scientists agree that the ancestors of the whales were land mammals that returned to the sea. But just what mammals these ancestors were no one knows. Some authorities see similarities between the early whales and the archaic carnivores, the creodonts.

Whales also resemble the sea-going reptiles, the *Ichthyosaurs*, to an astonishing degree, and both the aquatic mammals and the aquatic reptiles look like fish. The similarity between all of these groups is often cited as a striking example of convergent evolution. It shows that the strict limitations of life in the sea impose similar adaptations on dissimilar animals.

The fossil record for whales is spotty. However, one early Cetacean giant, *Zeuglodon*, is well represented in fossils. This creature, with its sixty-foot body, pointed snout, and wicked-looking teeth, is the image of the classic sea serpent of sailors' tales. When the

Zeuglodon

notorious Dr. Koch, the fossil forger, obtained some *Zeuglodon* fossils, he strung several of them together and called the result a sea serpent.

The original discoverer of *Zeuglodon* was confused by the remains. He thought the creature was a marine reptile, so he called it *Basilosaurus*, which means "king lizard." Later it was renamed *Zeuglodon*, which means "loop tooth," a more prosaic but more accurate name.

Paleontologists assume that the whales developed torpedo-like bodies early in their evolutionary history. Modern whales are hairless, and it is probable that this too represents an early adaptation, for hair creates resistance in the water which slows down an animal's swimming speed. The whales handle the problem of keeping warm by having developed a thick layer of fat or blubber to take the place of hair as insulation.

The whale's front legs are modified into flippers and the back legs have disappeared entirely. Long muscles run the length of the whale's body and tail to provide the power for the tail which propels the whale through the water. One unique and unfish-like adaptation is that the tail ends in a horizontal fin or flukes that move up and down. Fish have a vertical fin that moves from side to side. The flukes are stiff and strong, but entirely fleshy structures containing no bones. Another fleshy structure is the dorsal fin that helps stabilize the body.

Cetacean evolution has proceeded along two lines, the toothed whales and the baleen or whalebone whales. In the second type the teeth are unimportant or absent. The mouths of these whales are lined with plates of fibrous material that strains tiny animals from the water. This is baleen or whalebone. *Zeuglodon* was a toothed whale and most closely resembled the modern dolphins. But the real giant—the giant of giants—is found among the baleen whales. This is the great blue or sulphur-bottom whale, the biggest creature that has ever lived.

The statistics of the blue whale are staggering. It can weigh 150 tons. The largest extinct dinosaurs weighed a paltry fifty tons and the largest land animal today, the elephant, tips the scales at an insignificant six tons.

At birth a whale calf is about twenty-three feet long and weighs two tons. Newborn whales are quite well developed, as they must be to survive in the sea. When a young whale is weaned at the age of seven months, it weighs twenty-three tons. This means that on its mother's milk the whale has been able to gain 200 pounds a day! Unsurprisingly, whale's milk is very nourishing, containing 38 per cent fat. (Actually, the growth statistics are not as astonishing as they first appear; some seals grow even faster proportionately.)

After weaning, the whale continues to grow at the rate of nearly ninety pounds a day until the age of four when growth slows down. The whale's food consists entirely of small shrimp-like crustaceans that whalemen call krill. When the blue whale is feeding it opens its lower jaw, which serves as a huge bag, to collect the krill. Then it closes its jaws, and the water is forced out through the fringed plates of whalebone. The krill are caught in the fibers and make a meal for the giant.

The blue whale and the other baleen whales have been able to attain their enormous size because they are amazingly efficient users of the food resources of the sea. The oceans teem with tiny plants and animals of various types. These are lumped together under the name "plankton." A host of tiny creatures, including the red shrimp-like krill, make up the animal plankton, which feeds upon the plant plankton. In the traditional food chain of the sea each creature is eaten by a slightly larger creature.

The whale shortcuts the food chain by eating great numbers of tiny animals. Baleen whales are the only large carnivores which can exist this way. Fortunately for the whale, krill are plentiful and easy to catch. Sometimes the bright red krill are so densely packed that they give the ocean a reddish hue over an area of hundreds of square miles. It is in such "fields" that the great whales "graze."

The blue whale is sometimes called the sulphur-bottom whale, a name descriptive of its yellowish underside. The yellow is not the whale's skin color; it comes from a thin film of tiny plants which normally grows on the whale's belly. The whale's back, however, is a bluish black; hence, the more common name of blue whale. During the nineteenth century, the blue whale was "discovered" many times by many different people and given many different names. The proliferation of names has been reduced, but there is still some confusion. In Europe the whale is called *Balaenoptera musculus*, whereas in the United States it is *Sibbaldus musculus*.

Whalemen of the last century could not hunt the blue whale—it was much too fast for them. With its mighty tail it could easily speed through the water at ten knots, and could cover shorter distances at even higher speeds. Powered whaleboats still have trouble overtaking a speeding blue whale.

Besides being unable to match the speed, the nineteenth-century open-boat whalers considered the blue too big to handle. If they managed to kill one, it would sink. It was also too violent, for a wounded blue whale could easily wreck a whaling boat.

But technology caught up with the blue whale. In the course of about ninety years of modern whaling some 350,000 blue whales have been killed, mostly in Antarctic waters. Because of its size, the blue whale has been the most intensively hunted whale of modern times.

The old-time whalers hunted right and sperm whales, and hunted them practically to extinction. After a while there were not enough of these whales left and the industry began to falter. Technological advances like the harpoon gun allowed whalers to expand their catch to include the larger and faster whales—the fin whale, the humpback whale, and the blue whale.

Although whaling has provided copious statistics concerning the weight and size of dead whales there has been little study of the

Blue whale

habits of living whales. The blue whale migrates over great distances, but we have only a vague idea of what route it takes. In summer the blue whales can be found in the high Arctic and Antarctic latitudes, although they are far more common in the Antarctic. They feed on the swarms of krill that grow in the wake of the retreating ice. Blue are believed to swim farther into polar regions than any other species of whale.

By autumn the blue whales are again in temperate waters where mating takes place. Babies are born ten or eleven months later, after the whales have spent summer in the Antarctic and again returned to warmer seas. Adult whales are insulated from the cold waters by a thick layer of blubber. Newborn whales have only a thin layer and would quickly freeze to death if born in icy waters.

It is really hard to imagine the immensity and grandeur of the blue whale. Photographed from the surface, only a portion of the whale is visible. No one has yet succeeded in taking an underwater photograph of a living blue whale. Washed ashore, as they sometimes are, blue whales and all other large whales are helpless hulks that quickly suffocate. But in the water this giant is the picture of grace. Its smooth body glides effortlessly through the depths.

Being mammals, whales are air breathers. When traveling, the blue whale will come to the surface once every ten or fifteen minutes to breathe. It takes in air through its blowhole, a specially adapted nostril on the top of the animal's head. When the whale exhales the warm air from its lungs, it condenses in the colder atmosphere in just the same way as our breath condenses on a cold day. A whale has a lot of breath and the cloud of condensation can be seen for miles. This is the whale's telltale "blowing" from which the expression "Thar she blows!" comes.

We don't know accurately how deep the blue whale can dive; it probably does not dive as deeply as the largest of the toothed whales, the sperm whale or cachalot (*Physter catodon*). There is no need for a blue whale to dive deeply since the tiny crustaceans that are its food live quite near the surface. The sperm whale, however, is adapted for eating bigger prey. This whale's diet consists almost entirely of large squid. Although these creatures are very numerous they live deep in the ocean and rarely come to the surface, so the sperm whale must dive for them. No exact measurements of the sperm whale's dives have been made, but one sperm whale became entangled in a submarine cable, 3,200 feet beneath the surface, and drowned. Most authorities believe that the sperm whale can dive even deeper if necessary.

The sperm whale grows to a length of eighty feet. It gets its name from the misconception that the oil found in its head is sperm; it is not. The whale's other name, cachalot, comes from a French dialect word, *cachau*, that means large tooth, a notable feature of this whale.

The whale family is not only the giant in size of the animal world; whales may turn out to be the mental giants as well. The small toothed whales like the dolphin have always been considered intelligent. Over the last decade, as scientists have been able to study these attractive creatures closely, they have turned out to be even more intelligent than anyone had expected. Some dolphin enthusiasts claim that the dolphin is more intelligent than the chimpanzee, the most intelligent of the great apes.

Are the giant whales—the blue and the sperm—as intelligent as the smaller toothed whales? The sperm whale has the largest brain that has ever existed on earth. The total weight of an animal's brain is not a true measure of its intelligence, for an elephant has a larger brain than a man. But an elephant is much larger than a man. The ratio of a man's brain to his total body weight is about 50 to 1, whereas with an elephant the ratio is closer to 1000 to 1. The dolphin has a more favorable ratio. It has a larger brain than man and although it weighs 300 pounds its ratio of body weight to brain weight is a respectable 90 to 1. The blue whale, on the other hand, has such an enormous body that its brain ratio is a staggering

8,500 to 1. But body to brain ratio is not everything, for the humble mole has a better ratio than man does. It is reasonable to assume that all whales, including the giant blues, are intelligent creatures. At present there is no way of knowing for sure. The problems involved in trying to test a creature 80 or 100 feet long seem insurmountable. Even casual observation of the activities of these giants is limited.

We are not at all sure how the blue whale finds its way around. Its eyes are tiny, and not well developed. That doesn't matter much because it could not see very far underwater even if it had good eyesight. There is no indication that the blue whale has a well-developed sense of smell. If it is like the toothed whales, the blue whale's primary sense is hearing. Dolphins have an echo-locating

Sperm whale

126

system for finding their prey. Scientists have discovered that at least some of the baleen whales are constantly emitting sounds. It is probable that they find their way around by a form of echo location or sonar, just as submarines do. Whalers agree that the great whales possess an acute hearing ability.

Is the blue whale the ultimate in giantism? Not necessarily. Before whaling, the blue whale was biologically successful. Food was plentiful, and the oceans vast. There is no reason to believe that whales would not continue to evolve until they reached even more gigantic size. Now their future may be cut short by the appearance of a highly efficient predator—man.

10

Death of the Giants

THERE ARE certain advantages to being a giant. Life is more placid. A large plant eater is safe from most predators. A healthy adult elephant has nothing to fear from a tiger.

The giants can get food often denied other animals. A giraffe can reach the leaves on the top of a tree, the elephant can knock the tree down, and then eat the leaves. A small antelope can do neither. If there is a local drought large animals can simply migrate to an area where conditions are better. Long journeys are difficult and dangerous for small animals.

It takes a prodigious amount of food to feed a giant mammal. In the wild, elephants must spend upwards of sixteen hours a day eating or looking for food. But curiously, the problem of getting enough to eat is less acute for giants like the elephant and the whale than it is for the tiniest of mammals, like the shrew. Pound for pound, tiny mammals produce more energy, need more heat, use more oxygen, breed faster, and die younger than large animals. Therefore, pound for pound, they need more food.

The blue whale weighs 30 million times more than the long-tailed shrew (smallest of the shrews) and eats a ton of food a day. This is less than one hundredth of the whale's total body weight. But the shrew must consume an amount of food equal to its own weight every day. If forced to go ten hours without food a shrew will die. Large mammals can go for days or weeks without eating.

There are some obvious disadvantages to giantism too. An

128

animal may simply outgrow its potential food supply. Some giants may be too clumsy to move effectively. An elephant might be unable to get out of a hole that a mouse could scramble out of with ease or that an antelope could have cleared in a single jump.

Even if food were plentiful a gigantic plant-eating mammal might find that there were just not enough hours in the day to chew an adequate supply. Dinosaurs grew larger than land mammals, but we have to remember that cold-blooded reptiles did not need as much food per pound of body weight as warm-blooded mammals.

The giants breed more slowly. The elephant has the longest known gestation period—twenty months. The rhinoceros is second, with eighteen months. Giant mammals usually have one or, at the most, two offspring at a time. Therefore, the giants must depend on a high individual survival rate rather than on enormous numbers to maintain their species.

The disadvantages of giantism outweigh the advantages. No giant-sized animal has ever been as biologically successful as the lowly opossum, which first evolved while the dinosaurs were on earth. Today's opossum has changed very little since the age of dinosaurs. While giant mammals in North America have been eliminated or confined to parks and reserves, the opossum is prospering and extending its range.

By any criteria the most numerous and successful order of mammals is that of the rodents. It is also the one order that has produced almost no giants. One exception was *Castorides,* a beaver the size of a bear that lived in North America during Pleistocene times. The largest known rodent was *Dinomyidae* from South America which was the size of a small rhinoceros. Neither of these giant rodents survived long.

A statistical analysis of mammals that have become extinct since the end of the age of dinosaurs shows that something like 40 per cent of the groups of large mammals have survived as against over 60 per cent of the groups of small mammals.

Although the extinction of large mammals is common enough, so many of them became extinct at one time—the end of the Pleistocene or Ice Age—that many scientists believe that something very strange happened.

Alfred Russel Wallace, the man who along with Charles Darwin first systematized the theory of evolution, wrote in 1876: "We live in a zoologically impoverished world, from which all the hugest, and fiercest, and strangest forms have recently disappeared . . . yet it is surely a marvelous fact, and one that has hardly been sufficiently dwelt upon, this sudden dying out of so many large Mammalia, not in one place only but over half the land surface of the globe." We now know the extinctions took place over the entire land surface of the globe.

The most dramatic wave of extinctions occurred in North America when the Pleistocene epoch ended 10,000 years ago. The mammoths, mastodons, giant ground sloths, horses, camels, saber-toothed cats, giant jaguars, dire wolves, giant beavers, several species of musk ox and bison—all in all, about one hundred species of large mammals vanished.

Stranger still, their ecological niches were left empty. No new large animals moved in to replace those that had died out. Herds containing a single species of bison expanded to fantastic sizes, but

Size comparison of six-foot man (far right); *Baluchitherium,* largest land mammal; giraffe, tallest living land mammal; elephant, largest living land animal;

this was an unnatural or at least unusual situation. In Africa some twenty species of large animals share the grasslands. In America the grasslands became dominated by a single species.

The history of the horse gives the best illustration of the problems posed by the Pleistocene extinctions. Horses evolved on the North American continent. Then at the end of the Pleistocene the horses, along with so many other large mammals, died out in North America. But the horse did not die out in Asia. Ultimately man in Asia domesticated the horse. In the sixteenth century, thousands of years after the last native horse had died, the Spanish conquistadors reintroduced the horse to North America.

Some of the Spaniards' horses escaped. These wild or, more accurately, feral horses (a feral animal is one that has been domesticated but has returned to a wild state) flourished in the homeland of their ancestors. Their near relatives, the feral burros, did equally well. The horse's habitat had not disappeared when the horse did. Why, then, did the horse die out in the first place?

One thing is certain; it did not freeze to death. The weather was actually getting warmer across much of North America when the horse became extinct. Besides, many of the animals which disappeared, like the woolly mammoth and the woolly rhinoceros, had developed during the Ice Age and were superbly adapted for sur-

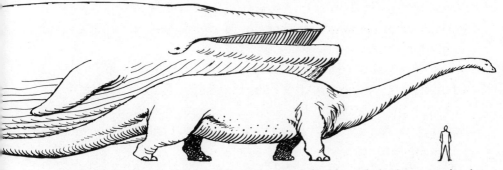

sauropod dinosaur, largest of the dinosaurs; and the blue whale, largest animal of all time.

vival in severe cold. Most of the large mammals that died off had already lived through several glacial advances and retreats. The woolly mammoth should have been able to follow the glaciers back to the north, as it had done before. There is no obvious reason why it should not still be living in the Arctic.

Both giant herbivores and giant carnivores died out at the end of the Pleistocene, but the mystery of the extinctions concerns only the plant eaters. Once the herbivorous giants were gone the large carnivores quickly followed their prey to extinction. A saber-toothed cat could not exist on rabbits and prairie dogs, and even the bison was no replacement for the mammoths and giant sloths.

What happened in the rest of the world? In South America the reduction of giants was, if anything, even more severe than in North America. Giant sloths and glyptodonts, toxodonts, and *Macrauchenia* all passed into oblivion. In South America today there are no giant mammals and relatively few large ones. Compare the animals of South America with those of Africa. Both continents contain extensive tropical areas and vast grasslands. Both should be able to support a roughly comparable variety of large animals. At one time they did. But they do not any longer.

The Eurasian continent lost its mastodons and mammoths, its "Irish elk" and giraffe camel, its woolly rhinoceros, and many other giants and near giants. However, the large Eurasian mammals seemed to survive better than those of North and South America. One species of elephant, two species of rhinoceros, plus horses and camels continued to flourish.

Australia was cut off from the rest of the world, yet it still seemed to experience a wave of extinctions that wiped out its largest mammals near the end of the Pleistocene. The most notable victims in Australia were *Diprotodon*, a rhinoceros-sized marsupial, and the giant kangaroo.

Africa looks like the one shining exception to the general rule of extinction of giants at the end of the Pleistocene. Africa today contains the world's greatest collection of giant land mammals. Many scientists believe that Africa somehow escaped the mass extinction of the giants. But other scientists denounce this as a "rose-colored glasses" view of African wildlife. One of the most severe critics is Dr. Paul S. Martin, a geologist and biologist from the University of Arizona who has taken a special interest in the problem of Pleistocene extinctions. Dr. Martin says that the large animals of Africa today represent "only about 70 per cent of the species that were present during the late Pleistocene. Thus, while the proportion of African mammals that perished during the Pleistocene was less than that in North America, the loss in number of species was still considerable. In addition to the large mammals that now inhabit the African continent, an imaginary Pleistocene game park would have been stocked with such species as the stylohipparion horse, antlered giraffe, a giant sheep, and an ostrich of larger size than is known at present. In Africa, as in America, the wave of Pleistocene extinctions took only the large animals."

Many explanations have been offered for this mass death of giants. One is that the extinctions were caused by disease epidemics. During much of the Ice Age, glaciers formed a wall of ice between the North American continent and the Eurasian continent. Animals that had once migrated freely from one to the other were blocked from doing so. Throughout the period of isolation, animal populations of the Old and New World became adapted to different diseases. When the ice melted and the animals of the two continental land masses could again mix freely each population infected the other with its own diseases.

Disease would strike hardest at the large herbivores, for they usually lived in herds and germs could spread more quickly among them than among animals that lived solitary lives. Large animals would also be more sensitive to the long-term effects of disease. Because they breed so slowly it would be a long time before the individuals who died off in an epidemic could be replaced.

Camel

imperial mammoth

However, most scientists do not feel that disease was the major reason for the Pleistocene extinctions. While it is possible that one or two species were wiped out by epidemics, most experts have looked to other causes. The majority of scientists feel that some sort of change of climate was the major factor behind the extinctions, but there is no general agreement on what sort of change it was.

John E. Guilday of the Carnegie Museum in Pittsburgh, Pennsylvania, believes that at the end of the Pleistocene the world got drier. As the land dried up two things happened: First, many habitats, like the swampy forests that served as home for the mastodon

Long-horned bison

Giant sloth

Smilodon

Dire wolf

Animals of North America during the Ice Age

in eastern North America, simply disappeared; second, the more severe conditions forced many large animals which previously had lived in harmony into competition for the reduced food supply. Large animals, he feels, would be the first to suffer as conditions deteriorated.

The American bison survived by getting smaller, Guilday believes. "The bison survived this time of stress," he says, "and had no trouble recovering and flourishing . . . as demonstrated by the unnatural spectacle of millions of individuals but of a single species."

Bob H. Slaughter, a paleontologist from Southern Methodist University, believes the killer of the giants may have been longer, colder winters. Large animals have long gestation periods and fixed breeding seasons. If winters got longer the young animals would have been born during the late winter when green vegetation was not available. Small mammals with short gestation periods and flexible breeding seasons could await warmer weather before mating, and their young would live.

But some scientists think the giants could have survived a climate change. Says Dr. Martin, "We know that they [the large mammals] had witnessed and certainly survived the advance and retreat of earlier glacial ice sheets. And among today's large mammals most are remarkably tolerant of different types of environments. Some large desert mammals can endure months without drinking; others such as the musk ox live the year round in the high Arctic. Reindeer and wildebeest migrate hundreds of miles to pick their pasture. Why should we believe that the great mammals of the Pleistocene were less adaptable?"

Dr. Martin is chief spokesman for a group of scientists who believe that the extinction of the giants was brought about by the introduction of a new predator into the world—man. While man remained in a primitive state he was no more effective a hunter than the saber-toothed cat; indeed, he was probably a good deal less effective. But armed with the weapon of fire man became no ordinary predator; he became a superpredator, with enough power at his command to destroy huge herds of large mammals.

How could prehistoric man, a relatively small and weak animal, have been responsible for the extinction of so many giants like the mammoth? A possible answer is provided by a reconstruction of a mammoth hunt that took place 10,000 years ago at what is now Dent, Colorado.

The Dent hunt site was discovered in 1932 after a cloudburst washed away part of a gully near South Platte River. The erosion exposed a concentration of mammoth bones. Scientists from the Denver Museum sorted out the bones and found that they represented the remains of eleven immature female mammoths and one adult male. Mixed in with the bones were three flint arrowheads and some boulders that seemed to have been deliberately moved into the area.

C. Vance Haynes, Jr. of the University of Arizona reconstructed the following scene: "The mammoth bones were concentrated at the mouth of a small gully where an intermittent stream emerges from a sandstone bluff to join the South Platte River. It seems plausible that here the . . . hunters had stampeded a mammoth herd over the edge of the bluff. Some of the animals may have been killed by the fall; others may have escaped. Those that were too badly hurt to fight free of the narrow gully may have been stunned with the boulders . . . and finally dispatched with spear thrusts."

Evidence of mass kills of mammoths and other large mammals by prehistoric hunters has come from many sites throughout the world. Killing an adult mammoth or other large animal may have been an impossible job for primitive hunters armed only with stone-tipped spears. But a small band of hunters armed with fire could stampede a herd of large animals over the edge of a cliff, either by chasing the herd with lighted torches or by setting a brush fire.

Mass killing of this sort would have been extremely wasteful. More animals would have been killed than could possibly have been used by the hunting band. Dr. Martin has called this kind of hunting "Pleistocene overkill." The problem these prehistoric hunters faced is that they may have had to kill off an entire herd, or at least a large part of the herd, in a stampede, in order to kill any individual animal.

Overkill theorists believe that the survival of the musk ox, a large shaggy and easily hunted animal of the far north, offers dramatic evidence to support their ideas. Dr. Martin notes that the musk ox once inhabited the northern portions of the Eurasian continent, but was exterminated there. However, it survived in Greenland and

Hunters using fire to stampede mammoths over a cliff

parts of the Canadian Arctic, because these areas were isolated by glaciers from the bulk of North America. The hunters were unable to reach the musk oxen living in this refuge. By the time these ice sheets melted and musk oxen from Canada and Greenland did come into contact with man, the men were no longer those wandering superpredators, but the Eskimos. "The Eskimo," writes Dr.

138

Martin, "had the good fortune, or good sense, to harvest musk oxen on a sustained yield basis, and the species was able to spread westward through Northern Canada, ultimately recovering part of its Alaskan range. If the woolly mammoth had also occupied the Greenland refuge, it too might have survived the Pleistocene."

Dr. Martin thinks he can relate the waves of extinction on each continent with the first appearance of man, or at least with man's discovery of the use of fire. As an example, the extinctions in Africa began some 40,000 years ago, about the time the first traces of human camp fires are found. He says flatly, "In no part of the world does massive unbalanced faunal extinction occur without man the hunter on the scene."

Opponents of the Pleistocene overkill theory are numerous. They point to Africa where for the last 20,000 years primitive hunters have lived off big game without exterminating a single species until the introduction of modern weapons.

The complex problem of the Pleistocene extinctions involves biologists, geologists, and anthropologists, and the astronomers have also stepped forward with theories of increased cosmic ray bombardment as the cause of the mass deaths. Another astronomical theory is that the energy output of the sun changed in some way and produced the climate conditions that led to the extinctions.

And so the argument goes on. Unless someone invents a time machine, the cause of the Pleistocene extinctions will probably remain clouded in mystery forever. But whatever the reason, or combination of reasons, our world today is sadly depleted of giants. What the future holds for those that remain is the subject of the next chapter.

11

Future of the Giants

IN 1834 TWO Eskimos hunting on Bering Island in the Komandorskie group located near the Bering Strait of the North Pacific reported seeing a large, lean, seal-like animal which they could not identify. The Eskimos were quite familiar with seals, sea lions, walruses, whales, and other animals native to northern waters. This creature, however, was strange to them. The Eskimos may have been the last men on earth to see a living specimen of one of the vanished giants of the sea, Steller's sea cow (*Rhytina stelleri*, literally "Steller's wrinkled one," a name given for the animal's folded skin).

Steller's sea cow was a close relative of the tropical manatee and dugong. It looked like a seal but in reality was a distant relative of the elephants. Steller's sea cow was the giant of its kind reaching thirty feet in length and weighing up to three and a half tons.

The giant sea cow was discovered by naturalist Georg Wilhelm Steller who sailed with the great explorer Vitus Bering. Bering was employed by the Russians to explore the northernmost limits of the Pacific Ocean and to see if North America and Asia were connected. This voyage of discovery turned into a disaster. Disease broke out among the crew, food ran short, and Bering himself died.

On November 4, 1741, Bering's starving and sickly crew brought their ship, the *St. Peter*, to a landfall on a remote and uninhabited island. The crew had been hoping to sail all the way back to Siberia but there were not enough able-bodied men left aboard to handle the ship, so in desperation they dropped anchor at this desolate spot. It was under such dramatic circumstances that Steller discovered the great northern sea cow.

These slow-moving peaceable giants grazed on aquatic vegetation that grew near the shore. They had no enemies until man found them. The giant sea cows were easy prey even for Bering's weakened men.

After a few weeks the men of the *St. Peter* had recovered their strength and continued the trip to Siberia. They carried with them the valuable pelts of sea otters and blue foxes taken from the Komandorskie Islands.

During the next quarter century hunters flocked to the islands. They came close to exterminating the sea otter, and they succeeded in killing off the giant sea cow. Steller's sea cow was not valuable for its pelt; it served merely as an easily caught source of food for the hunters. There had probably been no more than a few thousand of these giants at the best of times.

Some animals once believed to be extinct have been found alive. Under strict protection they are being brought back from the edge of extinction. But there seems no hope that the story of Steller's sea cow will have this sort of happy ending. These animals were too large and their eating habits kept them too close to shore for there to be any possibility that a band of them have escaped detection for over a century.

What is remarkable is that Steller's sea cow is the only giant mammal known to have become extinct within the last 500 years. Certainly some large animals—the zebra-like quagga, for example —have become extinct in recent times. But the quagga cannot properly be considered a giant.

Steller's sea cow was unique. It was not merely a separate species; it was so different from its nearest relatives that it had a genus classification all of its own.

Compared to the mass extinctions of the Pleistocene, the modern record is not too bad, particularly when one considers the destructive potential of firearms and man's ability to alter the landscape and destroy an animal's natural habitat. But the age of giants is over and those that remain depend entirely on man's good will and good sense for their continued existence.

Unlike some small animals—rats, for example, which compete successfully with man and defy all his efforts to exterminate them—the giants cannot compete anymore. Fortunately, during the twentieth century we have begun to adopt a different attitude toward animals, at least the rarer and stranger animals, and attempts are being made to preserve them. Unfortunately, these attempts are sometimes too little and too late.

In 1775 a Russian mining engineer named Peter Jakovlev recognized that the giant sea cow was being killed off at such an alarming rate that there would soon be none left. He petitioned the authorities to order its protection. But no one was interested, and within a few years the animal was gone. Similar warnings about other animals have been and still are being ignored.

The next giant that will almost certainly follow Steller's sea cow into oblivion is the Javan rhinoceros (*Rhinoceros sondaicus*). A few years ago there were so few individuals of this species left that they may already have died out. Certainly there were not a sufficient number of these creatures alive to make the possibility of a comeback more than an idle wish. Another East Indian variety of rhinoceros, the Sumatran rhinoceros (*Didermocerus sumatrensis*), is almost as rare. This species may continue until the end of this century, but its survival beyond that point is doubtful.

The great Indian rhinoceros (*Rhinoceros unicornis*) is a fairly common zoo resident. It is larger than the other Asian rhinos. The male may be fourteen feet long, stand six feet at the shoulder, and weigh over two tons. The horn of this giant is fairly small. Its skin is studded and folded, giving the animal the appearance of wearing a heavy suit of armor. Continued survival for this spectacular ani-

Steller's sea cow

mal, at least in the wild, is doubtful, for the wild population is now
down to a few hundred individuals. It has, however, been successfully bred in captivity and may survive as a zoo species.

The white rhinoceros (*Diceros simus*) is even larger than the
great Indian rhinoceros and is the largest living rhinoceros. Its
weight may reach three tons. Not only does the white rhinoceros
possess the greatest bulk of the remaining rhinoceros clan, it also
has the largest horn. It is smooth skinned (for a rhinoceros), lack-
ing the armored look of the great Indian rhinoceros. Despite its
name, this animal is not white. The name seems to have derived
from a mispronunciation of the Afrikaans word *weit*, meaning
wide. Although somewhat more numerous in the wild than the great
Indian rhinoceros, the white rhinoceros is still so rare that its survival can be assured only by the most rigid protection. It has not
yet been bred in captivity.

Only the black rhinoceros (*Diceros bicornis*) of Central and

143

Southern Africa has a good chance for long-term survival. It is the most numerous in the wild, and breeds most readily in captivity. But even the black rhino will require strict supervision and can live only in game preserves or national parks.

When you consider that these five species are all that remain of the magnificent rhinoceros family which was once represented from the tundra to the tropics, and contained among its members the largest land mammal, you can get a fair idea of how far the giants have fallen. The elephant is more successful than the rhinoceros, but among these giants the decline has also been startling. Throughout history there have been over 300 different kinds of elephants and elephant-like creatures. In the late Pleistocene there were at least seven distinct representatives of the order Proboscidea. Today

Javan rhinoceros

there are two. (Most authorities recognize two types of African elephant, a rain forest form and a bush form. But these are so much alike they are regarded as variations of a single species.) The Pleistocene range of the Proboscidea was world-wide. Today they live only in tropical portions of Asia and Africa.

In some parts of Africa elephants are numerous enough to represent a danger to agriculture. But it is inevitable that in the not very distant future wild elephants will be confined to national parks and game preserves. Even now, poachers who slaughter elephants for the ivory of their tusks are a threat to the elephant population.

Of the two remaining species of elephants the Asian or Indian elephant (*Elephas maximus*) is the smaller, rarely reaching a height of ten feet at the shoulder. The Asian elephant also has proportionally smaller tusks and ears. More docile than its African relative, the Asian elephant is the one seen most often in circuses and zoos. Asian elephants have been domesticated for centuries. Representations of domestic elephants have been found among the artifacts of the Harappan civilization, the earliest known civilization of India. These artifacts date back 4,500 years. The Asian elephant is still used as a beast of burden today, although one may assume it will someday be replaced by modern machinery.

The Asian elephant provides less of a temptation to modern hunters than the African variety. Its relatively small tusks (five or six feet long at most) yield less ivory. And an Asian elephant with its small ears and gentle face makes a poor, almost pathetic, trophy when mounted upon a hunter's wall.

The giant tusker with the enormous flaring ears is an African elephant, the largest living land mammal. A large bull may stand eleven feet at the shoulder, have eight-foot tusks, and weigh more than six tons.

Although stories of dangerous "rogue" elephants abound, the African elephants generally lead a peaceful existence. They travel in herds of twenty or thirty, industriously searching out the several hundreds of pounds of vegetation each elephant needs every day.

Behind the elephant but rivaling the largest rhinoceros in size comes the hippopotamus (*Hippopotamus amphibius*). An adult bull hippo stands about five feet at the shoulder but its bulbous body often gives it a weight of four tons. The hippo was once fairly widespread but now is confined to rivers and estuaries in tropical Africa. There it thrives remarkably well. The hippopotamus is protected from hunters throughout much of its range, but in some areas the numbers of these giants have become so great that conservationists actually have to kill off a certain percentage to keep them from overruning their food supply.

The hippopotamus spends most of its time in the water, and its diet consists largely of water plants. But it can also be surprisingly agile on dry land and will undertake long inland excursions to find suitable food. These foraging expeditions often end in farmers' fields; hence, the need for controlling the size of the hippopotamus population.

So long as it is protected the hippopotamus will probably get along well in the modern world. It is doubly fortunate, for unlike the elephant which is a temptation to poachers, the hippo has little commercial value and illegal hunting of this giant is rare. If all else fails the hippo can survive in the zoological parks of the future. It takes well to captivity and breeds freely. Hippos have been known to live for nearly fifty years in the zoo.

The giraffe (*Giraffa camelopardalis*) is the tallest animal alive today. Size gives it several advantages. The obvious one is that it can overtop all the other browsing animals to get to the higher leaves on trees. The giraffe's great height also gives it a good vantage point from which to look out for possible danger. Its eyesight is excellent and when it spots an approaching predator it can run away at great speed.

The giraffe is another of the African giants that is doing fairly well under protection. Its spectacular appearance, which renders it a valuable tourist attraction, will probably assure its survival for the foreseeable future. In any event, it breeds easily in zoos.

Although there has been a tremendous amount of recent interest in man's closest living relatives, the great apes, we have been astonishingly careless about protecting them. Of the two giant apes alive today, the orangutan (*Pongo pygmaeus*) of the forests of Borneo and Sumatra is probably doomed to extinction, at least in the wild state. There are only a few thousand left. Although they are supposed to be protected they are still being killed and captured. Orangs are difficult to keep in captivity, but they have been bred in zoos. Future generations may know them only as zoo animals.

Chances for the gorilla (*Gorilla gorilla*) are better. There are actually two types of gorilla. The lowland gorilla is still fairy numerous and probably will survive. The mountain gorilla, which was only discovered in 1910 living in the high forest-covered mountains of the Congo, is rare. Perhaps there are fewer than 10,000 of them today, but no one is sure.

The gorilla has become considerably more popular over the last few years. It was once regarded as a King-Kong type of monster, but recent field studies have shown that these giant apes are peace-loving, rather shy animals. They adapt readily to captivity and quickly develop a strong attachment to their keepers.

The largest of the land carnivores today are the grizzly and Kodiak bears, both thought to be giant races of the more common brown bear. Although still reasonably numerous in North America, the grizzly bear is in trouble. It has not been able to adjust to living in close proximity with man, even though it is protected in many of the areas where it lives. In recent years grizzly bears have made unprovoked attacks on campers in national parks. With more and more vacationers crowding in on grizzly bear territory the outlook for the bear's future is cloudy, unless scientists can learn enough about the grizzly's habits to devise methods of adequately protecting it and the people who may be nearby.

The effect that prehistoric hunters had on the giant mammals of the land is disputed, but there can be no disputing the fact that modern man has had a near fatal effect on the giant mammals of the sea.

The two giants among the seals (the order Pinnipedia, "the fin-footed ones") have been endangered by hunters. Largest of the Pinnipedia is the southern elephant seal. An elephant seal bull can grow to a length of twenty feet and a weight of 8,000 pounds. The name of this seal comes not only from its elephant-like size, but from the long proboscis of the males, although the elephant seal's proboscis is nowhere near as long or useful as an elephant's trunk. The southern elephant seal was first discovered at the beginning of the eighteenth century, but hunting did not really begin until the middle of the nineteenth century. By the end of that century the numbers had been so severely reduced that the sealing industry almost disappeared.

When the hunters went away the elephant seal population began to recover, but then the hunters returned. This time, however, sealing was strictly controlled and the population of southern elephant seals has actually increased somewhat since regulated hunting was begun in 1910.

The northern elephant seal is smaller than its close relative to the south. The large bulls reach a length of only sixteen feet. These seals used to breed abundantly along the Pacific Coast of the United States and Mexico from San Francisco Bay southward for a thousand miles. No one knows how many of these seals there were at the beginning of the nineteenth century. In 1885 the northern elephant seal was thought to be completely extinct. Then in 1907 a herd of 100 was found on the coast of Mexico at Guadalupe, a small beach backed by cliffs 3,000 feet high. The northern elephant seal has been totally protected since 1922, and the species has begun to recover.

Both types of elephant seals have been kept in captivity, but

Elephant seal

neither has been induced to breed. Their continued existence depends on the effectiveness of their protection in the wild.

Just below the elephant seal in size is the walrus. Bulls may be ten feet long and weigh more than a ton. The tusks grow to lengths of over three feet and weigh up to twelve pounds. Tusks of the female walrus are usually two feet or less. The famous walrus moustache consists of 400 or so stiff bristles. These are extremely sensitive and the walrus uses them for feeling its way about in dark waters; it also uses them for shoveling food into its mouth. Clumsy as it may appear out of the water, the walrus can scoot across the ice with remarkable speed. Its speed is equal to that of a running man, as more than one surprised hunter has discovered.

The walrus was once very numerous in Arctic seas and it has been hunted by Eskimos for centuries. Commercial hunting began in the nineteenth century and by the beginning of the twentieth

Walrus

century the walrus had become so rare that it was no longer worth-
while for commercial hunters to pursue it.

The walrus population has risen a bit from that low point. Today
there are somewhere between 45,000 and 90,000 walruses in the
Arctic. Eskimos still kill 6,000 a year but this has brought about
no appreciable decline in the walrus population.

In captivity the walrus has proved extremely popular. Unfortunately, although walruses seem to be perfectly happy in captivity,
they have not yet been bred in captivity. A lot more must be discovered about the walrus before it can be considered a successful
zoo animal.

Of all the giants, however, man has been most ruthless to the
largest of them all—the whales. The blue whale is not only the
largest living mammal, it is the largest creature that has ever lived.

For this reason, if for no other, it deserves to survive. For the very same reason it may not.

A hundred years ago thousands of blue whales roamed the seas. Today there are probably fewer than a thousand blue whales left. Other giants like the sperm whale and the finback are similarly threatened. International whaling is supposed to be regulated, but the regulations do not always work. A major problem in whale protection is that the great mammals swim in international waters, and although many—even most—countries would like to protect them, for regulations to be effective all countries must agree to protection. Unanimous agreement has proved impossible to obtain.

Another problem in setting adequate regulations on whaling is that no one can be sure what adequate regulations are. So little is known about the total number of whales in the world and their breeding habits that trying to decide the level at which whaling can be maintained without reducing a species of whale to the extinction level is just guesswork. The only real answer to the preservation of these great creatures is total protection of all large whales. Whale oil, whalebone, and other whale products can easily be replaced by substitutes. These greatest of all giants can never be replaced.

We can now see that despite their formidable bulk, the giants of ancient and modern times were peculiarly vulnerable creatures. Man has played out the old story of David and Goliath with the giant mammals many times, and every time, as little David with his slingshot, man has won an easy victory. The time has now come to put away the slingshot—forever.

Suggested Further Reading

Carrington, Richard A. *Elephants*. New York: Basic Books, Inc., 1959.

———. *A Guide to Earth History*. London: Chatto & Windus, 1956.

———. *Mermaids and Mastodons*. New York: Rinehart & Co., 1957.

Colbert, Edwin H. *Dinosaurs: Their Discovery and Their World*. New York: E. P. Dutton & Co., Inc., 1961.

———. *Evolution of the Vertebrates*. New York: John Wiley & Sons, Inc., 1955.

———. *Millions of Years Ago: Prehistoric Life in North America*. New York: Thomas Y. Crowell Co., 1959.

Darling, Lois and Louis. *Before and After Dinosaurs*. New York: William Morrow & Co., 1959.

Fenton, Carroll Lane. *Tales Told by Fossils*. New York: Doubleday & Co., Inc., 1966.

Hellman, Hal. *The Right Size*. New York: G. P. Putnam's Sons, 1968.

Holden, Raymond. *Famous Fossil Finds*. New York: Dodd, Mead & Co., 1966.

Ley, Willy. *Dawn of Zoology*. Englewood Cliffs, N. J.: Prentice-Hall, Inc., 1968.

———. *Exotic Zoology*. New York: The Viking Press, 1959.

Maxwell, Gavin. *Seals of the World*. Boston: Houghton Mifflin Co., 1967.

Scheele, William E. *The First Mammals*. New York: The World Publishing Co., 1955.

Slijper, E. J. *Whales*. New York: Basic Books, Inc., 1962.

Spinage, C. A. *The Book of the Giraffe*. Boston: Houghton Mifflin Co., 1968.

Wendt, Herbert. *Before the Deluge*. New York: Doubleday & Co., Inc., 1968.

Index

INDEX

INDEX

Mammoth, 98-105, 108, 130, 132, 136-137
  imperial, 98, 99
  woolly, 99, 100, 102-103
Mammuthus imperator, 98
Mammuthus primigenius, 99, 100
Man
  Java, 114
  Neanderthal, 111
  Peking, 113
Mantell, Gideon, 27
Marsh, Othniel Charles, 20, 55-56, 58, 76
Marsupials, 50-52, 61, 132
Martin, Paul S., 133, 136, 137-139
Mastodon, 27-28, 90, 92, 94-96, 130, 132, 134
  American, 94-95
  beak-snouted, 94
  long-jawed, 90, 92
  short-jawed ("true"), 90, 94-95
Mazurier (surgeon), 14-15
Megaceros, 82, 84-85
Meganthropus, 115
Megatherium, 63, 66-67
Mesozoic era, 38, 42
Mexico, 16, 148
Miletus, Greece, 17
Miocene times, 72, 74, 80, 85, 94
Missouri, 27
Missourium, 27-28
Moas, 117
Moeritherium, 88-89
Mole, 126
Mongolia, 59, 71, 94
Monotremes, 48, 50
Moropus, 79-80
Mosasaurs, 42
Multituberculates, 50
Mylodon, 68

Neanderthal man, 111
Nebraska, 81, 94
New Zealand, 117
Noah, 19

Odyssey (Homer), 17
Og, 19
Oligocene times, 76, 78, 105, 108
On the Genealogies of the Gods (Boccaccio), 18
Opossum, 50, 52, 129
Orangutan, 147
Order, 39
Orestes, 16
"Origin of Species, The" (Darwin), 33-34, 37
Osborn, Henry Fairfield, 71
Ostrich, 117, 133
Overkill theory, 137-139
Ox, musk, 100, 130, 136, 137-139

Paauw, 118
Pakistan, 71
Palaeoloxodon antiquus, 96, 98
Palaeomastodon, 89-90, 92
Paleocene age, 59
Paleontology, development of science of, 32-37
Paleozoic era, 38
Pampas, 36
Pangolin, 69
Pantotheres, 50
Patagonia, 68
Patriofelis, 58-59
Pausanias, 17
Peking man, 114
Pennsylvanian age, 48
Perissodactyls, 75-76, 79, 80
Permineralization, 40
Phenacodus, 52-53
Phiomia, 89-90, 92
Phylum, 39
Pig, 80-81
Pinnipeds, 113, 148
Pithecanthropus, 114
Placentals, 50-52, 61
Plankton, 121
Plater, Felix, 13
Platypus, duckbill, 49

INDEX

160